BUSINESS BY NUMBERS

Learn to love the figures that will make your company grow...

Garry Mumford

I dedicate this to my wife Thelma. Without her support and patience, I never would have achieved what I have.

CONTENTS:

Section 2: The 15 basics of business finance 83

Section 3: Valuing your future 131

AN INTRODUCTION:
Set your SatNav to the future

" A **good plan** is like a **road** map: it shows the **final destination** and usually the best **way** to get there. "

H. Stanley Judd

There are lots of business books out there. **Thousands**, in fact... books to make you more focused and more successful, books to make you richer quicker, and (quite possibly) happier in ways that you haven't dared to imagine.

Some of them are actually very good and not unreasonably priced. Some even go as far as delivering on the promises they make on the cover!

So, if you're leafing through this in your local bookshop, why should you shell out your hard-earned money to buy mine... and (more importantly) spend your hard-won spare time reading it?

1. This book is designed specifically for all of you who really don't enjoy the single most important part of running a business that will actually determine whether or not it succeeds: **the numbers**.

2. What you're getting with this book is an easy-to-follow guide on how to put the financial and administration systems in place to ensure that your business not only grows to its full potential, but actually makes a healthy profit along the way (and no, the **two** aren't the same thing).

3. To make it even easier, the book is neatly divided into bite-sized, **numbered** chunks – so you can **do everything (literally) by numbers...**

Every business owner is busy, so just read **one** section at a time, inwardly digest... and see how quickly you move from being someone who shies away from budgets, balance sheets and spreadsheets to someone who can **turn the numbers** in their business **to their advantage**.

The end result? A company that someone will pay handsomely for, or an enterprise that your family can continue to run long after you have embarked on a world cruise, or retired to the golf course.

Either way, that's well worth the cover price and a few hours of your time.

And if the very words **financial**, **administration** and **systems** send shivers of cold dread down your spine, relax. I've written this specifically for people who are far happier harnessing their creative and entrepreneurial skills than counting the beans.

As long as you know where you want to go, this book will help get you there.

What's inside...

Over the last **25** years, I've helped countless businesses achieve their potential by setting down straightforward guidelines to give structure and security to their operation. These guidelines mean they can evolve without the growing pains normally associated with companies as they grow.

This book follows a similar pattern.

Inside you'll find **three** distinct sections.

1. sets out the approach you will need to adopt to fulfil the growth potential of your venture.

2. is a simple and practical guide to the basics of business finance, recognising that not every business owner is as fond of finance as I am. While you may well be able to delegate many, or even all, of the finance functions in your business to someone better qualified than yourself, you should **always** understand what is going on.

3. is where it gets really interesting. Having absorbed (and put into action!) all you've learned so far, you may well be considering cashing in your asset at some point in the future – obviously at a far higher price than you'd achieve today! This section focuses on how you create value in a business – critical if ever you want to raise capital, or sell it for the highest possible price.

SECTION 1: Growing your business to its full potential

> " Your **present** circumstances don't **determine where YOU can go;** they **merely** determine where you start. "
>
> Nido Qubein

Where do you want your business to be **five**, **10**, **20** years from now? Whether your plans are to end up in the FTSE 100 or something more modest – you shouldn't set off without some idea of how you're going to get there.

This section sets out the basics you need to put in place, from explaining the difference between profit and cash, through to setting out the level of financial information you will need to drive your decision making.

You'll learn how to choose the right software, the best way to create a budget and even discover the difference between an accountant and a finance director.

There's also a diverting description of a heritage steam railway – which is far more relevant to a modern business than you might think.

1. Is your business an infant, an adolescent or an adult?

" Life is like riding a bicycle. To keep your balance, **you must** keep **moving.** "

Albert Einstein

Spoiler alert! Anyone who has read E. Gerber's superb *The E-Myth Revisited: Why Most Small Businesses Don't Work And What To Do About It* will recognise a lot of the thinking from that book on these pages.

That isn't an admission of plagiarism, not least because I readily acknowledge the influence Gerber has had on the way I look at business. He has helped to shape a whole generation of businesses and inspired several shelves full of business books.

If I can make a suggestion, I very strongly recommend that you make *The E-Myth Revisited* your next read.

Where this book differs from Gerber is in focussing on the principal weaknesses that many owners will admit to when it comes to managing finances, and providing simple ways to overcome them.

1. Most who go into business do what they know best – providing services or making products that they have a firm grip on. The problem is that they end up also having to undertake the tasks they aren't necessarily good at or trained to do.

2. They may then do those things badly or, more worryingly, not at all. Managing money is often one of those things we like to avoid. Yes, many people go into business to make money, but they don't necessarily know how money works.

3. The result is that, at a certain size, the business stalls. In Gerber's own words: "Most entrepreneurs are merely technicians with an entrepreneurial seizure. Most entrepreneurs fail because you are working IN your business rather than ON your business."

Like many of the best road movies, this book is not just about getting from A to B, but about growing up along the way... by working ON rather than just IN the business.

Gerber defines the **three** main stages of businesses as being:
1. infant
2. adolescent
3. mature

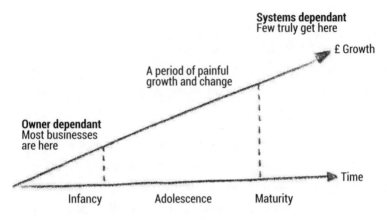

As you evolve and grow, your relationship with the world changes. More of that later...

Gerber also identifies the three characteristics required to be the perfect business owner:

1. the visionary entrepreneur
2. the systematic manager
3. the hands-on technician

In reality, very few of us manage to combine all of these qualities. Perhaps it's a question of the ways our brains are programmed, or just what presses our buttons.

I know, for instance, very few people who succeed in being creative, and organised, AND know how to install an RSJ or troubleshoot a software problem!

So, if your weakness is the managing bit, this book should prove helpful: it accepts that we can't all be good at everything, and sets out ways to deal with that.

Growing up in business

What are infant, adolescent and mature businesses? And why should it matter to you?

If you are a one-person freelancer, who has struck out on their own to run a small business doing what you love best (carpentry, tree felling, IT fixing, shopkeeping, beekeeping and so on) and you have no ambitions further than that, then you can probably get by perfectly well as you are.

You have no plans to grow, or employ more than a few people (if any), and when you retire you will simply close the business down – or pass it on to a relative or one of your employees perhaps.

You are, in Gerber's eyes, an infant business.

Many business owners are perfectly content to remain at that stage, because they enjoy the work and get a nice income. And there is nothing wrong with that. Unless you have ambitions to achieve more...

The problem with growing beyond the infant stage is that these businesses are highly dependent on their owner: their individual skills, personal contacts and experience are all locked into the business. If the owner falls ill, or retires, there is very little that a buyer will want to pay in return for taking the business over.

If the owner doesn't turn up for work one day, the business won't function properly. Eventually, it won't function at all.

Even businesses with a **£1 million** turnover and a **dozen** staff can be an infant business if the owner runs the whole shooting match, and they will probably see finance (and quite possibly administration) as a problem or challenge – something which gets in the way of doing the stuff they enjoy most.

This is at the opposite end of the spectrum from a mature business. People come, people go, and the work still gets done. It's systems dependent, not people dependent.

The mature business can readily be sold, because its value isn't tied up with any individual. The value is inherent in its systems. Indeed, if the owner doesn't turn up to work one day, the business should be able to function perfectly well. Their absence may not even be noted.

Every mature business will see the financial side of their operation as the opportunity to grow and become more profitable, rather than the problem holding them back... and will look for ways to make it even better.

n between infancy and maturity, just as in our own lifecycles, you have that awkward, messy, turbulent, exhilarating stage called adolescence.

It's often, but not always, associated with companies turning over around **£1 to £10 million**. These businesses have made a deliberate decision to break with infancy, and to function as an adult – but haven't quite got there yet.

Reaching maturity from this point means doing what many business owners find extremely problematic: learning how to let go, and allow other people to do the jobs you did at the beginning so you can concentrate on the really important, strategic decisions.

Just like when you strive to make the transition from infancy to adolescence (or from adolescence to maturity), you need to have strong support systems in place when you are developing your business.

Right then... are you ready to transform?

Systems mean service

To make the transition from infancy it is essential to make your business independent of you and your hands-on control. That requires you to put in rock-solid systems, so that everything's done exactly the right way – the way you want it to be done, no matter who's doing the job – every time.

Get it right, and it eventually becomes a smooth running machine, even in your absence... and possibly, particularly in your absence!

To make this happen, you need to ensure that the right technology, approaches and high standards are all in place.

This applies in every area:

1. marketing
2. sales
3. production
4. customer service
5. finances, too!

In fact, especially finances. A company can stumble along doing a mediocre job in most departments, but if you neglect the finances it will rapidly grind to a halt: the money doesn't come in, bills don't get paid, suppliers stop supplying and... well, everyone knows what happens next.

Money is the oil in the machine.

An infant business can get by while you do some of the bookkeeping yourself, take financial decisions without really referring to your financial reports, and put up with basic or old-fashioned accountancy software. You're pretty much running your business on intuition, or by the seat of your pants – like a pilot without access to instrumentation.

But can you imagine the owner of a **£10 or £20 million** company doing any of those things?

The big difference between an infant business and a mature business can be found in the controls that are in place within the finance department, together with the flow of information that is available to help shape every decision.

An infant business will have in-trays and out-trays (or possibly shoeboxes!) of bills to pay and customers to invoice, and sets of accounts that tell you how your company did last quarter or last year.

A mature business has the right people in place to manage their money day-to-day, using industry-standard accountancy software, and delivering regular, reliable, detailed financial reports that help you forecast and plan.

Three habits of mature businesses:

1. Spending more of their time looking forward than looking back.

2. Using all the information at their fingertips to make important financial decisions about the future of the venture — based on data, not intuition.

3. Utilising professional, not improvised, financial management.

The secret is not to wait until you're a **£10 million** company to have all of those things.

In fact, if you ever want to reach maturity, you need to develop these habits and put these structures in place now. They are an essential part of your transformation.

2. A steam railway fanatic's way of looking at business

> " It takes **as MUCH** energy to wish as it does to **plan.** "
>
> Eleanor Roosevelt

Please indulge me for a minute or two while I share one of my secret pleasures.

In my spare time I work for the Talyllyn Railway in Mid-Wales on the edge of Snowdonia. You may well have heard of it — or even enjoyed a trip on it.

Admittedly, they make use of my financial acumen rather than my abilities as a driver, wheel tapper or signalman (I act as their chief financial officer) but it allows me to feel part of something I really care about. And occasionally I'm allowed to stand on the footplate and pull the whistle.

For those of you interested in such things, these days it is billed as The World's First Preserved Railway, and provides **7.25** miles of sheer, steam-powered joy to **thousands** of visitors every year. But its original purpose has long since disappeared.

It was built in **1865** to carry slate from the Bryn Eglwys Quarry to the main line: in those days, Welsh slate was the roofing material of choice for millions of homes. The trains did their job perfectly well, chugging up and down the same **7.25** mile track. But, as it was a narrow gauge **one**, trains from the main line could not use it, and neither could its own engines venture onto the main line.

It served a single purpose and could only ever do what it was originally built for. When slate was no longer being shipped from the quarry, that purpose ended.

It couldn't grow and could never (in the analogy of this book) evolve into a mature business.

Now contrast that with the way the great railway builders went about creating our national network of tracks, connecting all of our major conurbations.

1. When they set out, they had a vision: a transport system that could grow without restrictions. For that, they needed a gauge everyone could stick to (not Brunel's wider gauge, sadly!), and a signalling system that all would understand and adhere to.

2. The introduction of timetables that everyone could rely upon (then, if not so much these days!) led to the standardisation of the time shown on our church clocks throughout Britain. Before then, there were regional differences reflecting the variations in the times of sunset and sunrise.

3. The systematic training of drivers, conductors, firemen and signalmen was introduced, and that meant that everyone knew their job and did it in the same way – again, a forerunner of many of the workplace practices we take for granted today.

What the great minds behind the railway revolution realised very early on was that to run a business that could be operated anywhere in the country, you needed systems and practices that could be applied every time you built more track, opened another branch line, added another station, built another locomotive or hired another worker.

Ultimately, that is what any business that plans to mature has to do… and it has to do it from **Day One**. You must say to yourself: "OK, today I'm only a small business, but the potential of my business is significant. I need to plan for its growth… NOW."

You need:

1. a business plan to follow
2. a budget to work to
3. a marketing strategy that can be financed and undertaken
4. accounting systems that let you predict, plan, invest and build

Anyone new coming into the business needs to know the operating procedures and everyone in the business needs (ultimately) to be dispensable so that the company can function perfectly well if they leave or the business merges, gets sold or taken over.

Of course, plans have to adjust to changes in circumstances, and new challenges or opportunities that come along, just as a sailing boat will tack if there is a change in wind direction. But you are doing just that – adjusting to circumstances – not constantly reinventing yourself. A much less traumatic process!

While today we often criticise our rather underfunded rail system, it was once the best in the world, and one of the foundation stones of the industrial revolution. It sparked the growth of the 'consumer society' we see today by transporting goods economically and quickly anywhere in the country. It was also the starting point for mass tourism.

Importantly, it was also the template upon which other nations designed and built their own rail systems – most use the UK's standard gauge... and you only have to travel on a high speed train in France or Japan to realise what properly planned and funded railway systems can be like.

3. What will your business look like when it's 'done'?

> "It's better to **look** ahead and prepare than to look back and **regret**."
>
> Jackie Joyner-Kersee

When I established my own business, Insight Associates, **25** years ago, I had a pretty clear idea of what it was going to look like today.

I knew approximately how many employees I was going to have. I knew what turnover we were going to reach. I knew what my role was going to be, over **two** decades later.

Was I incredibly prescient? Some kind of prophet? Sadly not.

The boring truth is that I had a very specific vision of what kind of business I was going to build. And then I went ahead and built it. My company looks the way it does today not by accident, but by design.

And that's how you should build yours, too. It all boils down to one question you need to be asking right from the start: "What will my business look like when it's finished?"

Look again at the three life-stages of a business — infancy, adolescence and maturity — and decide at the outset which of these stages your company will be at when it's 'done'.

Do you want to be a small firm with just **five** or **six** employees in one office, or do you want to grow into a much larger **£10 million** company with **50** employees, several branches, and (perhaps) even an international presence?

Do you want to be the head of a company that carves out a completely new niche in the global economy — a sector we haven't even identified yet?

As the CEO, do you want to be hands-on, or to sit back and take a more strategic view? Are you starting a business because you want a comfortable income, or are you looking to create an organisation which can go forward without you?

There's no right or wrong way, but if you don't already have those answers, you need to think about them — fast. This will allow you to lay the foundations for the future accordingly. In other words: if you want to be a successful company, start by behaving like one.

Building starts at the bottom

See it as laying the foundations for a building. Are you going to construct a shed, a skyscraper, or something in between?

If you want a lifestyle business, you'll be able to get away with simple systems and a simple infrastructure. If you aim to build a much larger company, you'll need to introduce the right processes, technology and people at an early stage.

A bigger company demands more effective financial management. This means thinking very early on about who's doing your accounting, what kind of information they're giving you, how useful it is, how you handle your invoicing, how you ensure your cash flow is smooth, and so on.

If finance and systems and administration are not your forte, you're probably not the right person to be bringing all this information together. You'll need someone by your side to do that for you – either as a key member of your management team or as a trusted consultant.

4. What's the difference between a bookkeeper, an accountant and a finance director?

I hear asked this question all the time – and even without being asked, it's one of the first things I explain to any client keen to 'grow up'. That's because it's the basis of putting in place the financial systems and controls required to take a business smoothly and (relatively) painlessly from infancy through to adolescence and then maturity.

Look on the **three** roles as **three** parts of a pyramid: at the bottom is the bookkeeper; in the middle is the accountant; and right at the top is the finance director.

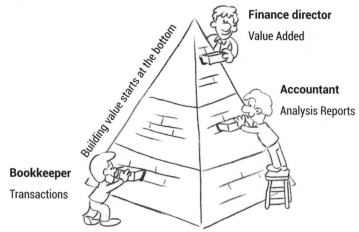

This isn't to undervalue the essential role that both the bookkeeper and accountant play in every business, or 'big up' the role of FD. Indeed, the bookkeeper is the foundation of your business, just as the lower level of the pyramid is the foundation that it rests on. So you can see from the size of the space they occupy in the diagram that they do a huge amount of the work too.

Bookkeepers manage all the sales invoices, all the purchase invoices and payments, they probably chase unpaid bills too – and perform a host of other unglamorous but vital roles. How vital? If the bookkeeper doesn't get all those transactions right, then the business will crumble. Fast.

In an infant business, they probably perform almost all of the financial functions required – except when the accountant steps in to check or file the VAT once a quarter, or even as little as once a year. The accountant checks and makes sense of what the bookkeeper has been doing, and perhaps fills in some gaps. They then run the reports off and get the accounts out.

So why would any business need more than that?

What the bookkeeper generates and the accountant checks are simply the bare, retrospective facts of how a business is running.

They process and record money coming in, money going out, money owed and money owing – figures that are at least several months old. They provide an historical record. Most small businesses are only able to analyse what has happened – and this only in very general terms.

Within a typical infant business, there is no data that will allow the business owner to have a better understanding of how to take their enterprise forward right away. Indeed, the very systems and software in use actually prevent that analysis from happening.

So now we reach the top of the pyramid, where the finance director comes in – either in the form of a member of the management team or as an outsourced consultant.

The top of the pyramid is where the value is truly added, where someone can insist on installing systems which provide data that lets them see where the business is, and where it's going, as well as where it has just been.

The FD role should help the owner make sense of the whole pyramid and understand the information needed to drive the business forward. They should challenge and question the other parts of the operation as well as help those other parts understand how finance functions and impacts upon the business.

The CEO/owner themself may be a financial whizz – in which case they can play that part too. But if they are either an entrepreneur or technician by nature, rather than a manager, they may struggle with analysing what the figures point to.

And unless you have someone acting in that role, your company will never evolve into a mature business.

Indeed, most people are pretty poor at running their personal finances – that's not my opinion, but the findings of successive surveys. Even so, quite a few of them go into business...

As Gerber points out, the temptation for business owners is to focus on the stuff they know, understand and enjoy, but they also have to cope with the aspects they are not so fond of: passing on responsibility at an early stage to someone who IS an expert is a key stage in evolving from an infant business.

That said, the business owner cannot totally abdicate responsibility for those areas: they need to have a firm grasp of what the FD is doing – and why – in just the same way as they should understand how the other cornerstones of the business function – such as operations and marketing.

Ask people why they went into business, and many will tell you that there is the potential to earn a great deal more, compared to being employed. But, ironically, many then look at the financial side of the equation as the boring part to be avoided.

They've got to shift from thinking, "Someone's got to do the books," or, "It's a pain in the neck, but someone's got to do it to keep the tax man or the bank manager happy," to realising that they themselves need to understand the flow of money within the business in order to make quality decisions and therefore increase their profit.

Every big business will see the financial side of their operation as the opportunity, and actively look for ways to improve on it.

So if you want to be a big business, it's time to start looking at finance as an opportunity rather than a challenge.

5. Why every ambitious business needs a finance director

> **“** Always **choose** people that are **better** than you. Always choose people that **challenge** you and are **smarter** than you. **Always** be the student. **”**

Sandra Bullock

If you're a small business, you probably think that hiring a finance director – someone trained, skilled and expert in making money an opportunity within a business – is out of your league.

"I can just about afford to pay my accountant – how on Earth can I invest in an FD?"

But turn that on it's head. Let's project where you might be in **five** years time, and you'll see why that FD role is so important.

If you're running a business with a **million** pound turnover, just imagine what it would be like running it with a **£100 million** turnover. You're sitting on your fat leather chair in your big office saying to yourself: "I've done it!" And outside your door is a long corridor, and at the end of that corridor, just around the corner is a door... with the word 'Finance' on it.

And on the other side of the door is an office full of bean counters. You've no idea what goes on in there. But you know you've got to have them, because someone has to pay the bills and all the other mysterious things that bean counters probably do.

Your conduit between those bean counters and your ability to make decisions in your business with a **£100 million** turnover is your FD – your candid friend, your confidante.

Your FD always has a grip on the **numbers**, and always understands the implications of what you're talking about.

Because they understand what's going on in that office full of bean counters, you don't need to.

When you look at any **multi-million** pound business, the FD is always just behind the frontman (that's you!).

If you want to be a **£20 million, £50 million, £100 million** business, think about taking on someone – perhaps in a part-time or outsourced role if the sums don't add up yet. But don't rely on your accountant to analyse your figures and advise you.

That's not their role, it's not what they're trained to do, it's not what you pay them for, and very few would position themselves as financial advisers. Critically, they are not close enough to the business to advise you.

An FD should more than pay for themselves in the value they bring to your business. And yes, a good one will cost.

All too often, people like me are brought into companies after a succession of increasingly expensive financial heads have passed through, each with an increasingly grandiose job title.

Each of them has been no more than a glorified bookkeeper or accountant. Each of them has been unable to fulfil the role of an FD. No single person is going to be content with daily processing AND adding value to the business. You either end up with the world's most expensive bookkeeper or the world's most inept FD.

An FD should be more than capable of having both an operational and strategic role within a business: yes, managing and controlling the day-to-day finances, but also developing and directing the financial strategy of a company.

Affording a full-time FD may well be beyond the reach of a small business... and they may not even need one. But there are plenty of skilled and highly experienced people offering their services in a part-time capacity. A day or two of their time a week, or even per month to begin with, may well be all you need to get your strategy and systems in place.

6. To become a big company, you need big company software

> ⁶⁶ **Excellence** is an **art** won by training and habituation [...] We are what we **repeatedly** do. Excellence, then, is **not** an act but a **habit**. ⁹⁹

Aristotle

So now you have an FD in place. Next you need to give them the tools to do their job.

Imagine that in the building next door, there is a business that is much larger than yours. It's the size of company you aspire to be. What things do they have in place that you don't, helping them sustain such a large operation?

Well, they probably have a lot more staff, who can handle a variety of roles, many more clients, bringing in more income, and a wider product range to sell.

They won't just be relying on having a broad grasp of how the company has performed financially in the last few months – information they could gain from a half decent accountant or even a good bookkeeper: they will know precisely where it's heading.

Their beating heart will be a sufficiently sophisticated accounting software system that – at the touch of a button – will transform its past and current financial transactions into a set of charts or tables that help them understand not only where the company is now, but where it could be if they played out a series of different scenarios.

Scenarios such as taking on more production capacity, entering new sectors, taking on more personnel, changing the pricing structure or investing in more marketing.

As your business gets more sophisticated, and moves from infancy to adolescence to maturity, you will need that quality of financial information. But unless you invest in that level of sophistication to begin with, you will never move beyond the early stages of development. It's the very foundation on which you build your business.

A **£10 million** business simply can't function with the kind of financial management they had when they were turning over **£1 to £2 million**.

Can you imagine trying to run **ten** branches of a clothing store, while waiting for your bookkeeper to get back to you about which suppliers are owed money – because they're on holiday? Or having no clue what your profit figures on each line you sell are?

No. All the **numbers** are at the fingertips of a mature business, because this is what keeps their operation running smoothly, avoiding nasty surprises and distractions.

More than that, this level of knowledge fuels growth. When they know their **numbers** inside out, they can take really informed decisions about future strategy, giving them an automatic advantage over smaller rivals who are, by comparison, in the dark.

They'll know how much they can discount to counter a rival; which products sell best in which stores or markets; even when and by how much they can risk raising prices.

The good news is that you don't have to wait until you are hitting **£10 million** to get the same kind of financial insight that gives the 'big boys' such a leg up. Indeed, if you are hoping to push beyond the **£1million** to **£2 million** level, you must develop a far deeper knowledge of your own financial data.

7. Five steps to becoming a mature business

> **"** It's not **what** you do **once** in a while;
> **it's** what you do day **in** and day **out**
> that **makes** the **difference. "**

Jenny Craig

So without further ado, here are **five** key steps that mature companies take to run smoothly and to grow.

1. Control your cash flow

- How much money is in your business account at any moment?
- How much money is going to leave your account, and when?
- How much are you expecting in, and when?
- Do you know the length of the cash cycle in your business?

In simple terms, that's how long it takes for money you spend with your suppliers to be returned to you by your customers (ideally with a profit attached!). Understanding the cash cycle is vital to predicting the cash flow in your business – and how much money it needs to run smoothly. Many viable businesses fail through a lack of cash. This is one element of what we call Working Capital.

It's important to know what may delay your cash cycle – and so prevent your business buying stock or paying vital bills. Your cash flow forecast should be at least as long as your cash cycle.

No matter how high your turnover, you need to understand when there's cash in your account, and when there isn't. This allows you to predict shortfalls and plan for them, and also to know when it is safe to invest.

Companies that simply assume that the cash is there because they are making sales end up with horrible cash flow problems – and eventually go bankrupt. By understanding your financial position on a daily basis, you will remain on top of your cash flow, and in better control of your business.

Action point: Make sure your accounts team gives you cash flow reports EVERY day (yes, **every** day!) This will give you amazing insight into how cash moves through your business, and allow you to plan much further ahead. And work out the typical cash cycle in your business – that too will tell you exactly how much money is tied up at any one time, and unavailable to pay bills or invest.

2. Know where your profit comes from

Mature companies know exactly which parts of their business make the most money – and which parts make the least.

They know which products or services sell at the highest margins; which customers are worth most to them (not in terms of turnover, but of profit!); which suppliers represent the best value for money; which branches, departments and employees are the cash cows; and which have relatively little to show for their efforts.

Mature companies use this information to decide which areas of their business to invest in and grow — and which to optimise or drop. Segmenting every area of your business in this way — profitable vs. non-profitable — allows you to concentrate on the things that make most financial sense, and grow much faster.

> **Action point:** Most of this information is in your accounts. Conduct a thorough analysis of what your main products or services really cost to deliver once you look beyond headline numbers, versus what they actually bring in. Repeat the exercise regularly — circumstances change, so don't rely on existing information, and don't assume you already know where the profit lies.

3. Benchmark yourself against your competitors

Larger companies have a really clear picture not just of their own financial standing, but of their competitors' too. They have detailed knowledge of how much their competitors are charging, how much they are turning over, and what profit they are making.

This helps them learn about which of their competitors' strategies are working, where the opportunities are, and where they need to play catch-up. By benchmarking themselves in comparison, they get a better idea of how well they are succeeding in their market. Businesses don't operate in a vacuum.

An in-depth understanding of how you are doing compared to your rivals helps you hone your business strategy.

4. Have a financial plan

Just as a **£10 million** company will have a clear business plan and a clear marketing plan, so too it will have a clear financial plan.

Financial goals for the next **12** and **24** months should be based on real data, not guesswork. And once you know where you need to be, work backwards to figure out how to get there.

If you are planning to increase profit margins by **3%**, what actions must you take now in order to make that happen? If you need to make something more profitable, what do you need to invest?

Leave nothing to chance – map out the actions necessary to help you reach your financial goals. You will have detailed, well-thought out budgets that enable you to fulfil your strategic goals. If you want to be a big company, start by acting like one...

5. Make sure your numbers help you take a long-term view

To really understand your company's financial position, it's not enough to know where you are today. You need to understand how your current position compares to that of last month, **six** months ago, last year, and **five** years ago too.

For example, you might be really pleased that you operated on margins of **5%** in February. But if you were operating on margins of **7%** in December and **8%** in October the previous year, that's a step backwards.

If, on the other hand, that's up from **4%** in December and **3%** in the October, it's a leap forwards.

When it comes to **numbers**, context – that is, trends over time – makes them meaningful. Companies that are scaling fast have a clear handle not only on where they are today, but also what the direction of movement is.

Action point: Good accounts should always show movement over time. Make sure yours do too. Without this kind of information, you risk making wrong decisions about your business, and your growth could be severely impacted. Get it right – and it will be far easier to move to **£5 million, £10 million** – and beyond.

8. Make sure you have the right accounting system to grow your company

"The single **biggest** problem in communication is the **illusion** that it has **taken** place."

George Bernard Shaw

A good accounting software system is at the heart of a thriving business; one that will deliver the sort of information you need to enable your business to grow... not hold it back.

So just what sort of accounting system do you need on which to build your **£10 million** (or **£100 million!**) business?

One, in short, that will not only do most of your work for you, but will also enable you to grow without the growing pains.

To illustrate my point, let me share a salutary tale.

A husband-and-wife team's business had reached a turnover of **£2 million**. But all that extra business meant hard work — lots of it. Every week, they would spend **three** full days ploughing through their accounts... themselves.

They had no free time, which was putting enormous stress on their relationship. They were drowning in paperwork. And they were struggling with a job they shouldn't have been doing, leading to mistakes and frayed tempers.

When told they could automate much of the process, the husband practically cried with relief. "The accounts have been dragging our whole lives down, but somehow we've never managed to delegate them," he said. "Getting rid of them would be an enormous burden off our backs."

What would they do with an extra **three** days each week?

"Concentrate on business development," they answered. "We'll be able to grow at a much faster speed."

What they experienced is quite common among businesses that have recently hit the **£1** to **£2 million** mark.

In the early days, it's relatively easy to keep track of your finances. As the owner, you might do this yourself, in Word or Excel. Or perhaps you worked with small bookkeepers who use simple accounting software or have built their own systems.

But as you grow, there is a lot more data to keep track of and it all gets more complex.

The trouble is, your financial management systems don't always grow in sync with the rest of your business.

I've seen so many companies whose workforce has rapidly expanded, that have doubled or tripled their client base and that have invested in new infrastructure such as offices and vehicles. Yet they handle their accounts exactly as they did when the owner worked out of their bedroom.

Some signs that you, too, have outgrown your financial systems:

1. Too much admin – every financial task takes ages and there is so much paperwork. You're doing things the longwinded way.
2. Bookkeeping is always out-of-date – because staff do not have time or capability to get it done on time.
3. Your company has grown to several divisions – but your accounting reports still only show one.
4. Too many short cuts – for example, there's just one line for 'Expenses' rather than a meaningful breakdown of what kind of costs you are incurring. The information isn't useful to you.
5. Too many steps – it's an effort, for instance, to raise an invoice or settle a bill.
6. Not accessible – directors who need easy access to accounts don't have it.
7. You haven't upgraded your accounts package – you're using an old version which isn't supported anymore and which keeps crashing. Or you have lots of systems which are simply not talking to one another.

If any of this strikes a chord, your finances are probably chaotic and stressful. Chances are, your accounts aren't ready when they should be, they're often wrong or incomplete, and they take up far too much of everyone's time.

In fact, you're lucky if there have been no major repercussions, such as missing money that you are owed, terrible cash flow, or suddenly facing a tax bill that is much larger than you expected.

To protect your company — and yourself — you need to upgrade the way you handle your accounts. Grown-up companies need grown-up systems.

How it got turned around...

Back to the couple at the beginning of this story. The first step was to introduce them to new accounting software. And, really, that was the turning point in their business, and their lives.

There are several programmes out there which you can use, depending on the point you have reached in your business and (most importantly) where you plan to get to at the end of your journey.

If you're only planning to drive **five** miles up the road, then an old banger or a low-powered small car might be as much as you need. If you're hoping to get up to John O'Groats, get the car you need for the journey BEFORE you set off. And it's the same with accounts software.

It shouldn't just handle accounting tasks: it will also need to tackle jobs like sales order processing, purchase ordering and stock control. That means it can be integrated into all aspects of your operation and will guide your decision making, not just provide helpful data for the people running the accounts.

Fit-for-the-journey accounts software has to have extremely flexible reporting, so it can provide a detailed understanding of a company's financial position.

Since knowing where you stand financially is key to making sensible decisions, flexible reporting is crucial if you want to grow smoothly.

One excellent add-on feature, which the better software programmes provide, allows you to scan data directly off purchase invoices, so there's no need to key them in, and no excuses from anyone who lets their expenses pile up!

A programme that integrates fully with Microsoft Excel and other popular systems will let you import and export data from a wide range of sources quickly and easily – helping to streamline your team's work.

So, in a nutshell: look for software that gives you all the capabilities the 'big boys' have – that will take the hard work out of entering new data, and that can be integrated into other parts of your operation. Anything less will hold you back.

Critically, it will provide the foundation stone for what I regard as the holy grail of business information...

9. The 'exciting world' of management accounts

" The **pessimist** complains about the wind;
The optimist expects it to **change**;
the **realist** adjusts the sails. "

William A. Ward

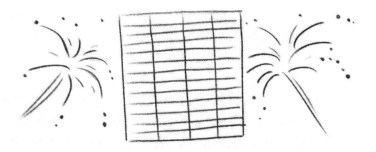

Every business owner knows about financial accounts... or they should do. They are a set of figures that (probably) your accountant prepares for you (possibly at the last minute) and which set out the headline figures of your previous trading year.

They are very important.

Indeed, preparing them and lodging them with Companies House is a legal obligation. You will also need them to support your Corporation Tax Return. And they will give you a snapshot of the way the business has traded over a given **12**-month period.

But — in most other respects — financial accounts are quite meaningless, especially for any business owner looking to make day-to-day decisions. In fact they can often raise more questions than they answer, telling you what happened – but not why. They certainly don't help you run your business any better.

Management accounts on the other hand are the holy grail of running a successful business. Let me explain the difference, so that you can prioritise having management accounts constantly available to you as you take your business into maturity.

First, what do good management accounts include that financial accounts do not?

The clue is in the title. They are called management accounts because they help you **manage** your business. Good management accounts provide context: enough detail for you to really understand what's going on, and help you make decisions. It's management accounts that will give you a true picture of your business.

Importantly, they should be presented in easily digestible ways – helping you to get the picture more quickly and memorably. They will also contain sensitive information that is for your eyes only, to be kept within the business, and they should be tailored to your needs.

Financial accounts, on the other hand, have to be produced in a prescribed way so they are pretty much the same for all businesses, they tend to be published publicly and people can get hold of them at Companies House. They tell you about what's happened in the past – and that's all.

Turning data into decisions

Even if you've never been in an aircraft cockpit, you can picture it: a tight space crammed full of hundreds of mysterious controls and displays, showing navigation information, engine information, speed, altitude, and so on.

No pilot would fly without this information, because it enables them to make good, safe decisions. Without it, they are flying blind, and risk crashing. And that's how I think of businesses that don't produce management accounts every month.

To make the right decisions you too need hard data, telling you what's really going on in your business. If you try to chart your course without the financial facts, you too are flying blind. You may not crash, but you're unlikely to get where you want to, either.

Your monthly management accounts report should be tailored to you, giving you the financial information you need not just to understand the past, but to navigate the future.

So what should they include?

Every management accounts pack must include the basic information you'd expect to see: a profit and loss sheet and a balance sheet covering things like turnover, gross margins, operating profit, overheads, cash in bank, debtors, and so on.

This raw data is made all the more useful if it is put into context through the use of percentages and other metrics that are readily understood. Data you can look at daily, and at a glance.

But that's not the really interesting bit...

Know your KPIs

Every business has, or should have, **key performance indicators** – data unique to them and which they need to monitor to know how well their business is doing against the past, market trends, their targets and quite possibly their competitors.

For example, one of my clients operates on very tight margins. If the cost of their raw materials moves even by 1%, their profit can be severely damaged. They need to keep an extremely close eye on this, so that they can adjust their pricing accordingly.

Another client is very dependent on **two** large customers. **One** of their key objectives for this year is to increase their customer base, so they are less exposed if one decides to source supplies elsewhere or to reduce their spending. Their management accounts track what percentage of their business these **two** clients are worth and report them regularly to the directors. Any significant shift will get flagged up early – giving them more time to respond.

What figures are crucial for your business? These are **your** KPIs.

Dive into the detail

Once you've established your KPIs, you need to dive deep and see what lies beneath the surface of each of them.

For example, a client providing training courses was having concerns around their profitability. Initially I tracked how profitable each category of course was each month. Over time, we all realised that this wasn't detailed enough. They needed to see the profitability of every single course they ran in order to make more informed decisions.

But in order to do that, they had to put more time into breaking down how each course was being run, and this involved changing the way they collected and analysed the raw data as it was entered into their systems.

Think: what kind of detail would be useful for your KPIs?

Show trends over time

Your figures are not meaningful until you can see them in some sort of context (as mentioned above). **£200K** in sales in January can be good if that's up from **£100K** last January, or bad if it's down from **£300K**.

You should be able to benchmark those figures against previous results, showing progress over time. You will also want to compare them to where you thought you'd be — those figures are in your budget. Use charts or graphs if necessary to make the material more readily digestible.

Project forwards

Your management accounts are not there simply to help you understand the past. They're there to help you manage the future (and the **two** are intertwined).

So set out on paper what you expect to happen over the next month or so. What do you already know about your cash flow? What do you already know about your KPIs?

Over time, you will learn what information is useful to you, and adjust your management accounts accordingly.

When I work with a new client I start with a monthly management accounts template, which is tweaked as I learn more about that client's business and their challenges. Over time the management accounts become progressively more valuable, helping clients understand what is happening in their business and therefore make better decisions.

This is the information mature businesses take for granted, and it's what smaller businesses need if they want to grow strategically.

Still anxious about understanding the information you're being given? Then the next section is just for you!

10. How to make sense of the numbers

> "There are **10** types of people in this world. **Those** who **understand** binary and those who don't."
>
> Jason Jones

Lots of business owners I know are far happier out on the factory floor, or drumming up work, than sitting behind a desk. Go one further and stick a spreadsheet in front of them and you might as well be asking them to translate hieroglyphics!

Not everyone is good with numbers, just as not everyone is great with reading or writing – including many high achieving business people. Some are just not interested in them. And that's fine too.

Some people's skill set lies in a different direction, and the savviest ones have the nous to make sure they have people around to pick up the slack. If this sounds like you, believe me you are not alone. And this whole book is intended to break down the barriers than many business owners have between themselves and numbers.

So here are **four** things your finance team can do to make your financial reports easier to digest:

1. Visualise. If you can't make head or tail of the numbers, ask your accounting team to present them as a graph, pie chart or in whatever form works best. Many people absorb information quicker this way.

2. Summarise. Ask for an executive summary of just a few key numbers, in a commentary. That way you get the information you really need without having to wade through figures that make your head spin. If you have any questions, you can always delve down into more detail.

3. Prioritise. Think about **three** to **four** 'numbers' that are problem or vulnerable areas for your business, or need monitoring closely – and get special reports on those. Is cash an issue? If so, ask for regular updates on who owes you money. Perhaps it's fuel or raw material costs? In which case, make sure you always have those figures at your fingertips.

4. Maximise. You've hired your finance team for a reason. Make full use of their expertise. Ask them to explain the figures to you rather than just dump them in your lap.

You don't have to become a financial expert overnight (or at all!). But you must help yourself become familiar with at least the basic numbers in your business.

To do otherwise represents unacceptable risk. Ignorance can be bliss, but it can also be fatal. A CEO who doesn't know what's in his or her accounts is like a ship's captain who's frightened of looking out of the wheelhouse window. There might be a great big iceberg just waiting to hole their ship below the waterline – which they could avoid, if only they see it in time – but how would they know if they don't look?

11. Why every business needs a budget – and how to set one

" Plans are **worthless,** but **planning** is everything... "

General Eisenhower

Although Eisenhower – the man who oversaw the incredible logistics of D-Day – was speaking in a military capacity, his words are just as relevant to your business's budget.

Too many businesses fail to give budgeting the care and attention it deserves – typically throwing together some optimistic figures and then promptly forgetting about them for the year. That's if they do them at all! I've worked with people who have actually told me: "I don't believe in budgets.".

Why? Probably because they don't really understand why budgeting can be so useful. They feel they need to do it, but aren't sure exactly what for. It's a common misconception that budgets constrain businesses. In actual fact they can help you achieve your goals. The true value isn't necessarily in the budget itself... but in the process of drawing it up.

As Eisenhower recognised, getting your head around the detail of how you achieve your objectives makes you look at every part of an operation – and see how each cog in the machine fits with the others.

He also recognised the need to make adjustments when circumstances changed. Indeed, he very nearly postponed D-Day because of bad weather. Had it been delayed, he had plans in place to deal with that too.

All those months and years spent working out exactly what was necessary to win the day paid off. The fundamentals were all lined up – the right troops, the right equipment and the right training in the right place at the right time. Then when changes to the plan were forced upon the Allies, they were able to respond.

Putting together a good budget for your business is exactly like that. And no, it needn't be as complicated as planning for an armed invasion of mainland Europe!

To come up with meaningful numbers, you must analyse your business in depth. While you may not get everything right, it will give you a better grasp of where you are headed, what success looks like, and help you recognise when things are going off track.

Budgets focus minds on what really drives a business and makes it profitable. They make you look at each part of your operation and assess how it is contributing to the success of the whole. They can also flag up which parts may be holding you back.

- Why are you pouring resources into a certain area of your business?
- Are all these activities really necessary?
- What do you need in place to achieve your growth goals?
- Are your growth goals realistic?

Only when you've answered these questions can you decide on what your final budget will be for the coming year, and how to allocate available funds.

So, try not to think of creating and managing budgets as an unpleasant task. Instead, see it as the perfect opportunity to review your business in depth – one which could be key to the success of your entire enterprise.

Of course, your budget is worthless if the figures it is based upon are no more than wishful thinking. Start with the questions:

1. What do we want to achieve?
2. How will we do it?
3. How much will it cost us to get there?

So, for example, if you want sales to rise by **20%**, what do you need to have in place? Do you need to hire **two** more sales people, buy a certain amount of equipment or give a particular department more funds?

When that happens, the end point – that **20%** rise in sales – is no longer a pie-in-the-sky dream, but the natural consequence of your game plan. And it becomes an entirely reasonable figure upon which to base your budget.

Don't get me wrong, optimism in business is great. It can sustain you through some of the darkest times your venture will face and if there's one thing for sure, every business will face some dark times. But when it comes to budgets, you don't need optimism. You need realistic, concrete plans.

Setting your budget

Here is a handy **five**-point guide on how to set a meaningful budget:

1. Know your goal. What do you want to achieve? Where do you want to be?

2. Create an action plan. With your goal firmly in place, formulate the actions needed to achieve it. What detailed steps will get you there, when will they need to be taken and how will you measure success? Then (and only then) can you produce your first set of numbers: a financial forecast. The forecast is the financial result of completing the actions. Most people do it the other way around: they start with their forecasted numbers and wonder how they are ever going to achieve them. It's all a load of wishful thinking.

3. Don't let a budget gather dust. It is a living, breathing, evolving entity which has to be constantly reviewed in response to changing circumstances. It's part of your day-to-day actions, your management reporting.

4. Visualise a budget road map. Where are you now? And where does your journey still need to take you? Sometimes your SatNav might direct you on a different route – but that doesn't matter as long as you are focused on your end goal, your destination.

5. Get your team buy-in. Now you've got your budget, you need to make sure that it's not just magic thinking. And the best way to do that is to get the whole of your team involved and on side – make sure they know what your goal is... and what contribution they can make to it.

Business is hard to predict. But if you find there's a significant difference between your budget and reality, then you need to understand why that's happening.

Think about how close you came to the budgeted figures, what adjustments need to be made, if any, and what changes should you make to improve performance.

> Budgeting is not a question of right or wrong, good or bad. It's simply a way to help you understand more fully what's happening in your business – a benchmark to measure performance.

I recommend you look at your budget at the very least quarterly, preferably monthly – but this could vary depending on the nature of your business. In an ideal world, your budget should be an integral part of your monthly management accounts pack – helping you to see precisely where you are in relation to your plans.

I'm often asked how long a budget document should be.

Many years ago I worked for a company in which my role was to generate the forecast figures that appeared at the end of a very large bound budget book: this was the 'bible' that set out in great detail the company's business plans for that year. The plans were an inch thick while the figures at the end were just a few pages long.

But the detailed thinking that went into those final few pages represented a guarantee that they were relevant and worth reading.

Making your budget meaningful also depends on sharing it with other people, not just keeping it inside your head.

12. Know the difference between profit and cash

"Worry is **interest paid** on trouble before it comes **due**."

William Ralph Inge

Profit does not equal cash! Obvious, yes? Well no, not for many company owners I meet.

In fact I'd say that it was the single biggest misunderstanding I come across... and it can be potentially fatal for a company – even one that is (on the surface at least) doing very well. In fact, these are the very businesses most at risk.

There's a simple solution: understand how a balance sheet works.

Time and again I meet business owners who run scared of balance sheets because they don't understand them. "All those figures dancing about in all those columns... give me the bottom line!" they cry. "How much did we sell? How much money did we make? Let me read the profit and loss account – I can get my head around that!"

But understanding the true financial picture is usually far more complex than that.

Remember: Profit is a **number** made up by accountants... and while the profit and loss account provides some valuable information, it is also not definitive. By that, I mean that it is – to an extent – subject to opinion. Moreover, it's only one part of a much more intricate story.

On the other hand, understanding the balance sheet is like taking the pulse of a business. It tells you exactly where you are at a given moment in time. And by seeing whether your pulse is running too quickly, putting the heart of your business in danger, it can flag up problems ahead.

Learn to love your balance sheet

Overcome your fear of all those figures in all those columns and you'll discover masses of valuable information sitting in the balance sheet which can put you in real control of your business.

A balance sheet consists of two halves: what you have and where it came from.

I like to put a client's balance sheet up on the big screen and explain what's going on. It then starts to make more sense. At a glance they can see how much stock they have, how much money they're owed, how much they have in the bank and so on... so they can begin to extrapolate what lies ahead – and plan accordingly.

So what IS the difference between 'profit' and 'cash'?

For me, the main issue to grasp with profit and cash is timing. Because (in 'accounting speak') we sometimes recognise profit well in advance of when the cash actually appears. You might have sold someone a pint of beer today and got their cash in your hand – but it's not until you pay your supplier at some point in the future that you can really see the profit.

Conversely, if you have sold a product to a customer who doesn't pay their bill quickly, you have a profit... but you won't be seeing the cash for some time to come. Why is it important? If you don't understand the difference, you could end up spending 'profit' that you really shouldn't because you will have bills to pay further down the line.

Stage 1: We invest **£50,000** into our new business. This is available as cash – and **£50,000** also becomes the money invested in the business, and so appears as that at the bottom of the balance sheet.

WHAT WE HAVE	Stage 1	Stage 2	Stage 3	Stage 4	Stage 5	Stage 6
Cash	£50,000					
Equipment						
Stock						
Customer Owes (Debtors)						
TOTAL	£50,000	0	0	0	0	0
WHERE IT CAME FROM						
Owners Funds (Share Capital)	£50,000					
Profit						
TOTAL	£50,000	0	0	0	0	0

Stage 2: We spend **£30,000** on equipment to run our business. So, we now only have **£20,000** available as cash in our business – but at that point in time we still have **£50,000** of value IN our business, although part of it has moved from cash to equipment – and so that continues to be the figure at the bottom of the balance sheet.

WHAT WE HAVE	Stage 1	Stage 2	Stage 3	Stage 4	Stage 5	Stage 6
Cash	£50,000	£20,000				
Equipment		£30,000				
Stock						
Customer Owes (Debtors)						
TOTAL	£50,000	£50,000	0	0	0	0
WHERE IT CAME FROM						
Owners Funds (Share Capital)	£50,000	£50,000				
Profit						
TOTAL	£50,000	£50,000	0	0	0	0

Stage 3: We invest **£15,000** in stock. We now have **£5,000** available in cash, but because we have stock and equipment, we still have **£50,000** IN our business.

WHAT WE HAVE	Stage 1	Stage 2	Stage 3	Stage 4	Stage 5	Stage 6
Cash	£50,000	£20,000	£5,000			
Equipment		£30,000	£30,000			
Stock			£15,000			
Customer Owes (Debtors)						
TOTAL	£50,000	£50,000	£50,000	0	0	0
WHERE IT CAME FROM						
Owners Funds (Share Capital)	£50,000	£50,000	£50,000			
Profit						
TOTAL	£50,000	£50,000	£50,000	0	0	0

Stage 4: We sell **£7,500** worth of that stock for **£15,000** to a customer who takes credit so does not pay us straight away, so this is where it begins to get complicated. At this point in time, we have the remaining **£7,500** still in stock; **£30,000** in equipment; **£5,000** left in cash; and a further **£15,000** in our debtors (the money the customer owes). So, our business now has **£57,500** of value on the balance sheet – **£7,500** of which is the profit and **£50,000** is our original investment.

WHAT WE HAVE	Stage 1	Stage 2	Stage 3	Stage 4	Stage 5	Stage 6
Cash	£50,000	£20,000	£5,000	£5,000		
Equipment		£30,000	£30,000	£30,000		
Stock			£15,000	£7,500		
Customer Owes (Debtors)				£15,000		
TOTAL	£50,000	£50,000	£50,000	£57,500	0	0
WHERE IT CAME FROM						
Owners Funds (Share Capital)	£50,000	£50,000	£50,000	£50,000		
Profit				£7,500		
TOTAL	£50,000	£50,000	£50,000	£57,500	0	0

Stage 5: Great news. A much larger customer comes along, and wants to buy lots of things from us. We go out and spend our remaining **£5,000** of cash on more stock – happy in the knowledge that we will sell it and our existing stock of **£7,500** for **£25,000**.

WHAT WE HAVE	Stage 1	Stage 2	Stage 3	Stage 4	Stage 5	Stage 6
Cash	£50,000	£20,000	£5,000	£5,000	£0	
Equipment		£30,000	£30,000	£30,000	£30,000	
Stock			£15,000	£7,500	£12,500	
Customer Owes (Debtors)				£15,000	£12,500	
TOTAL	£50,000	£50,000	£50,000	£57,500	£57,500	0
WHERE IT CAME FROM						
Owners Funds (Share Capital)	£50,000	£50,000	£50,000	£50,000	£50,000	
Profit				£7,500	£7,500	
TOTAL	£50,000	£50,000	£50,000	£57,500	£57,500	0

But our customer wants more, his order is for **£40,000**... but we don't have the cash to buy the extra **£7,500** of stock we need to satisfy all of his order.

WHAT WE HAVE	Stage 1	Stage 2	Stage 3	Stage 4	Stage 5	Stage 6
Cash	£50,000	£20,000	£5,000	£5,000	£0	£0
Equipment		£30,000	£30,000	£30,000	£30,000	£30,000
Stock			£15,000	£7,500	£12,500	£0
Customer Owes (Debtors)				£15,000	£12,500	£40,000
TOTAL	£50,000	£50,000	£50,000	£57,500	£57,500	£70,000
WHERE IT CAME FROM						
Owners Funds (Share Capital)	£50,000	£50,000	£50,000	£50,000	£50,000	£50,000
Profit				£7,500	£7,500	£20,000
TOTAL	£50,000	£50,000	£50,000	£57,500	£57,500	£70,000

Instantly our business looks like it's worth far more than it did when we set out – the grand sum of **£70,000** in fact. But that new customer too wants credit terms; so at that point on the balance sheet, we have no stock, **£30,000** in equipment, and we are owed **£40,000** from our customers. We have also made **£20,000** profit. While the business is worth **£70,000** on paper, some **£20,000** of which is 'profit', we have no cash left – and our customers won't be paying us for another **30** days. We also have a customer waiting for us to fulfil the rest of their order!

While we are now a 'profitable company', we have no cash. And we have a problem because we have no cash to pay our staff at the end of the month, or our rent.

Even though our business is worth more than we started with, and we have shown a healthy profit in the short time we've been trading, we won't be able to make use of any profit we have gained until our customers pay up.

The lesson

The example above represents a typical cash flow cycle within a company, except that it becomes far more complex in a very short space of time.

So you need to be prepared to:
1. understand the difference between cash and profit
2. not spend money in a business that's not there to be spent
3. have enough working capital to withstand the ebbs and flows of cash within a business, and/or
4. make sure you get your money in the door from customers quickly enough to keep your bank balance in the black

The more detailed section on cash flow goes into other ways to tackle this problem.

How balance sheets can predict the future

Now of course, keeping this balance sheet updated won't necessarily be the business owner's responsibility, but they should at least have an appreciation of how that balance sheet functions and the vital role it plays.

That's because it provides a useful snapshot of where your business is at any point in time. In particular, it will tell you how much cash you have in the bank, how much your customers owe (you might want to ask questions about that!), and what stock you have – raising the question of whether it is the right stock. It also flags up questions such as whether you are making full use of all the equipment on your balance sheet, and so on.

This data, combined with a cash forecast – projecting when money is going to come in and out of the door – will certainly help tell you if you have a problem looming.

I was recently able to advise a customer **18** months in advance that they were going to have a cash problem, simply because they were growing at such a rate that their debtors (the amount customers owed them) were increasing exponentially and tying up more and more working capital. Yes, they were hugely profitable, but you could clearly see the gap between cash and profit getting wider and wider. It's often the apparently most successful companies that most need to understand how a balance sheet works.

13. Get buy-in on your budget from your team

> "People rarely **succeed** unless they have **fun** in what they are **doing**."
>
> Dale Carnegie

Recently, at a conference, one of the presenters told a thought-provoking story…

A man was digging a hole in the road, surrounded by a group of people directing him. Each time he thought he'd finished they told him, "That's not where we wanted it, dig another one."

Before long, the street was littered with holes – and the man digging them was getting increasingly frustrated and annoyed. He had no idea why he was digging, so he saw the whole exercise as pointless.

Eventually, he asked why he'd been asked to dig a hole in the first place. And he was told that they were looking for the gas main, because there had been a leak. However, they'd lost the plans and had no idea where the pipes were.

Immediately, the digger's attitude changed. Now that he understood the relevance of digging the holes, he worked with renewed enthusiasm, and even made his own constructive suggestions about where it made sense to dig.

The moral of this story? If you want your staff to fully engage with what they do, and be more purposeful in their work, make sure they understand **why** they're doing what they're doing, its **value** and **how** it fits into the bigger scheme of things.

This is particularly relevant when it comes to your budget. Many companies have trouble getting their staff to take the budget seriously and stick to their spending limits and priorities.

A colleague of mine loves to relate how – in a relative's company – this became such a problem that he handed his staff Monopoly money. Every time they wanted to spend money for their department, they had to hand some over.

The point was to help them visualise their share of the budget, and make them more accountable for how it was being spent. It was certainly a creative solution!

But it's just as important to explain to staff why the budget looks like it does, and how their own portion of it fits into the overall strategy. Understanding where your piece of the jigsaw fits in is a very powerful motivator.

Without that context, the figures in the budget look random and abstract – especially if it is divided up in the plain, faceless way that so many companies insist on. With that context, it gains meaning and purpose.

So tell your staff how the budget helps your company achieve its goals. For example, if it's designed so that you have everything in place to raise turnover by **20%**, or to help you conquer a new target market. Then explain their part in the budget.

Tell them: "Your branch is getting £X in order to make it a flagship for the UK," or, "We're increasing your budget for communications training so that we can ensure the team works together seamlessly – and is ready to take the lead next year in a major project."

Do that, and not only will you have them fully on board with the budget, but – like our man in the hole – they may be able to make valuable suggestions about how to work within it, too.

14 . Systematise your business

> " [It's] **automatic**
> It's systematic
> It's **hydromatic**
> Why it's greased lightning! "
>
> *Greased Lightning* lyrics

Forgive me breaking into song, but these lyrics from *Grease* have a certain relevance here.

Quoting freely from Gerber, a business that runs on systems rather than relying on individual people is one that will be far more easily managed – and ultimately more successful. You can expand it, replicate it, or franchise it without the growing pains unsystematised businesses experience.

You can then sell it at some point in the future, and the new owner will know precisely what they are getting and how to operate the business just as successfully as you have. Personnel can leave without disrupting the business because the knowledge of how to perform important functions is not just locked in their heads.

Everyone automatically knows their role – and why that role matters.

Hydromatic? That's just another word for an **automatic** transmission (dating back to the **1950s** auto industry if you're interested!) – so no need to worry about changing gear as your car speeds up or slows down: everything is taken care of.

And, indeed, systematising your business could be likened to creating one of those wonderful Haynes car manuals that allowed you to maintain or repair your car (in the days before you needed a degree in electronics, and there was actually room under the bonnet to use a spanner).

Standard Operating Procedures

It all boils down to creating standard operating procedures (SOPs) for every part of your business, which – department by department – identify each function of your operation, and set out how they should be managed or undertaken – in detail.

Bring all these together and you have an operational manual for your business.

One entrepreneur, and another big Gerber fan, has successfully created operating manuals for each of his businesses, including hotels, and a care home which he later sold at a handsome profit. His manuals cover everything from the perfect way to make a bed through to how each guest should be addressed by staff.

Every member of staff knows what is expected of them, and every new member of staff can soon be brought up to speed.

Being as **systematic** as this can have a major bearing on one very critical aspect of a business: customer experience. Look at the big brands around the world – especially those in the service sector: their reputation has been built on customers knowing exactly what to expect, every time they buy one of their products or use one of their services. The big brands maintain that consistency of approach in all their outlets or market areas.

This goes back to Gerber's point that you should set your own business up as if it's the first venture in a future franchise that should operate like **greased lightning!**

So how does this translate to finance?

As this is a book about **numbers**, I'm focusing on those aspects of your operation where money enters the equation.

Having a documented process for every area impacting on your accounting might sound like hard work, or (at the very least) work for those who actually get pleasure from putting everything in neat rows. But it's an approach that generates results you can count on, and which will ensure that any operational decision you make is founded on facts, not wishful thinking.

And no, it doesn't have to be you who creates these manuals, although you may well need to oversee the process. One excellent way to empower your team is to involve them in producing the paperwork that drives their department along – but you will need to be the final arbiter on whether what they have produced fits the bill.

The instruction manual your business should generate would ideally include a detailed finance section that will cover everything that matters, for example:

1. who is on your bank mandate
2. who is authorised to make approvals and to what value
3. what forms should be used for each function
4. where things should be stored electronically
5. sign-off procedures
6. how to address queries
7. information on the security of data...

You get the picture?

In addition, you should define a monthly accounts action list that includes everything that needs to be processed or considered during that month.

This list can be broken down into main headings such as:
1. bank accounts
2. sales ledger
3. purchase ledger
4. cash book
5. nominal transactions
6. sundry items

And then each of these headings can be expanded into action lists tailored to each operation. Primarily they should include elements such as:

1. identifying bank items
2. coding approvals
3. bank reconciliations
4. expenses
5. petty cash
6. sending invoices and statements
7. chasing outstanding payments
8. payroll
9. handling credit cards
10. VAT
11. Corporation Tax
and (of course!)
12. what goes into the management accounts

I won't be too prescriptive here as each business will be run in a slightly different way, but every (and I mean **every**) aspect of managing the finances of your operation should be covered if this is to work properly.

15. Plan to succeed

" In the **absence** of clearly-defined goals, we become strangely loyal to performing **daily trivia** until ultimately we become enslaved by it. "

Robert Heinlein

Occasionally people ask me what is the biggest single step they can take towards gaining financial control of their business. And in this book I'm covering many topics – from cash flow and credit control to your relationship with your bank, and from systematising your finances to knowing when to upgrade your accounting software.

But if there is **one** overriding theme tune I can leave playing in your head, it's this: the importance of planning your finances.

Many entrepreneurs have a great handle on planning the key steps to growing their business... when to introduce new lines, when to move premises, even when to take on new personnel. But because of the inherent fear or lack of confidence so many people have around money, planning the financial side of things often gets pushed to the bottom of the to-do list.

Honestly, it needn't be that taxing. And here are some helpful tips to focus your mind on what matters... and why.

1. Plan your cash: So many good businesses fail because their leaders are caught by surprise when they run out of money. You must get to know your figures intimately. Make sure you know what's coming in, what's going out, when bills are due and what your cash situation is. I recommend a daily review of your cash position to help identify and deal with problems before they become urgent.

Securing your cash flow is the most important thing you can do – too many businesses go bust despite being profitable simply because they run out of cash.

2. Plan your budget: Plenty of companies set ambitious financial goals as part of their budget, for example a **20%** rise in revenue. Yet all too often, they have no real plan for how they are going to achieve them, so those goals simply remain wishful thinking. Understanding what action your business needs to take in order to fulfil its goals should be the basis of any good budget. If you know that to achieve a **20%** rise in revenue you'll need **two** extra salespeople, make sure that happens.

3. Plan your business: Build your business deliberately rather than allowing it to evolve haphazardly. Think carefully about how you want your business to look when it's 'done' – what kind of turnover do you want to achieve? How many employees do you want? Then put the right processes and foundations in place to ensure your company develops smoothly.

4. Plan for emergencies: Be a pessimist – plan for the worst financial eventuality. Make sure you have a contingency budget in place to ensure your survival in case the worst happens.

As you can see, financial planning is essential for both positive and negative reasons. It makes it easier to achieve your growth goals, and to function smoothly. It also help you pre-empt disasters that could potentially sink your business.

On a personal level, with good financial management in place, you will find running your business much less stressful.

When you're not constantly fire-fighting…

You will feel much more in control, and have more time to devote to other tasks that are essential for growth.

There is even value in the process of planning itself. Properly planning your financial goals, budget and cash flow forces you to look carefully at your business's priorities, structure, and the way it functions. You will learn a lot about your own company, and make better decisions as a result.

Five action points from this section to help your business grow:

1. Decide what sort of business you want to be running and where you want to get to: envisaging the destination will help you map the route.

2. Put standard operating procedures (SOPs) in place for every aspect of your business operation.

3. Invest in a software system that will take you the whole journey to being a mature company – and which will give you data you can use to see where your business **is**... not where it **was**.

4. Hire a Financial Director. Bookkeepers and accountants are very important people, but you will need someone (even part-time) to guide your financial decisions.

5. Set budgets that map out **where** you want to be, **when** you're going to get there, and **how** you plan to get there. You may very well need to change the plans – but the thinking you do will prove invaluable.

SECTION 2: The 15 basics of business finance

" The person who says it **cannot** be done should **not** interrupt the person doing it. "

Chinese proverb

Having got this far in the book, you'll now have a good grasp of the essentials of building a business that will stay the course. If you're unsure as to what individual aspects of running a business's finances entail, this section will provide the answers.

If you take on someone else to handle the finances of your business, they can be assigned the task of ensuring all these things happen. But as it's your business, you should – at the very least – have a handle on what all this means to your bottom line, and know enough to detect whether or not the job is being done properly.

As the leader of your business you cannot delegate all responsibility to other people.

Armed with this information, you need never be baffled by jargon again when you're talking to your finance team. You'll know what to ask from them to make your life easier, and your decisions more informed.

1. Manage your costs – don't let them manage you

You might think that the person who signs the cheques is the one in control of your company's finances.

Wrong. It's the person who places the order.

A few years ago, I was asked to work with a distressed business that had begun the process of formal insolvency as part of the rescue plan. While I was with the interim CEO in the call centre, surrounded by people with headsets busily talking to customers, he was approached by someone who wanted him to sign a cheque.

He screamed out: "I don't care who signs the cheques – who signed the (insert profanity here) purchase order?"

It had been a stressful time, so you can imagine how he was feeling. But what happened next went some way to explaining why his business was in trouble.

It turned out that someone in the company had ordered far more computer equipment for resale than was needed. But by the time the CEO was asked to sign the cheque, the merchandise was already in the warehouse. Because the CEO didn't have control over the purchase orders, he had no choice but to pay up.

If you've got to the stage of having to sign a cheque, it's already too late to start managing your expenditure – the damage has already been done. You will already be committed to making the purchase whether you like it or not.

And yet many companies are very strict about who signs the cheques (or more likely electronic payments these days), and not nearly strict enough about who places the orders in the first place.

As CEO, it is your responsibility to ensure that money is flowing through your company properly.

If this is a problem you recognise, it may be a good idea to take temporary control and sign off all orders yourself. That way you can see what employees are spending money on and how much, and if necessary challenge them in time to make a difference.

You may find that, even if they are spending money on reasonable items, they are spending at least some of it unnecessarily, buying too much or at the wrong time, or paying over the odds. Ask them to check the prices they've agreed to against those available elsewhere. There are plenty of businesses out there suffering because they're not getting the best deal on basic items.

Challenge everything, from paperclips to **£100,000** pieces of machinery. You will find that as soon as your team realises that their orders will be properly scrutinised, they will be much more careful about their orders themselves.

If your business is operating with slim profit margins, or none at all, then those savings could be incredibly important to the success or otherwise of the entire operation.

2. Business costs you should not accept

Recently, a client ordered a **£7,000** delivery to their office. When it arrived, the courier handed over the invoice: **£7,050**. They'd added on an extra **£50** for the delivery.

Worst of all, the client paid it without a second thought, even though it wasn't on the original quote or order.

This is where I let out my primal scream... it's louder than you'd like.

We all hate a rip off, and this is exactly what has happened here. The supplier snuck in the extra charge because they thought they could get away with it – and most people assume they have no choice but to accept.

In fact, this is just one type of cost every business has, but nobody accounts for. These can add up quickly, and before you know it, your overheads are out of control.

The good news is, most are avoidable.

Here are just a few:
1. Creeping costs: These are little charges that get added to a bill you've already agreed to, just like the delivery charge above. Another example might be a supplier telling you additional investment is necessary once you're halfway through a project.
2. Stealth price increases: All those regular expenses you pay such as electricity, gas and travel? The companies love to hike up your tariffs when you're not looking.

3. Additional costs you haven't considered: This is your own oversight. For example, if you're buying from outside Europe, you might forget you have to pay customs duty. Similarly, if you are not organised enough to collect your goods promptly once they reach port, the port can charge you (demurrage).

4. Suppliers passing on costs to you: A colleague used to work for a pharma company. If, when they imported their raw materials, there was a delay, they sent the materials by airfreight instead of shipping them — and passed on that cost to the client. I wouldn't have wanted to be on the receiving end of one of those bills.

So how do you prevent these costs spiralling out of control?

First of all, make sure they are no longer hidden. All the examples above can only happen because no one in the business is controlling expenditure properly.

There should be an approval process for all expenses, and every invoice goes through it — no exceptions. If you raise a **£7,000** purchase order and the invoice comes in for **£7,050**, it needs to go through the approvals process again.

As the business owner, ask to see all invoices from the last **three** months, and audit them.

1. Do you know what money is being spent on?
2. Do any of the sums surprise you?
3. Who's approving what?
4. Are existing procedures being followed?
5. Are there any additional costs (such as demurrage) you seem to be paying repeatedly, which can be prevented?

Then ensure that someone is held accountable for every penny you spend.

Second, challenge unexpected costs. That **£50** delivery charge? I'd have refused to pay it. The supplier is unlikely to give up on a **£7K** sale over the delivery charge.

This sort of saving, which will impact directly on your bottom line, will only happen regularly when your company culture encourages people to pay close attention to what they are spending.

3. Understand when you're making a profit

The difference between cash and profit is it the crux of many business's problems. And here is why...

So, you've just invoiced your clients for the work you did over the month. It was a good month – you've never been so profitable! For a long time, you've sworn that when you have enough cash, you'll invest in a new piece of equipment that will push your business forward. Should you go ahead and buy it?

Obviously there are many variables here so this is an impossible question. But until you see that cash in the bank, you can't count on it ever materialising. It may look like you're in profit, but that's just theoretical until your clients actually pay up, and your money is safely in your account. If that didn't occur to you, you're not alone.

Many business owners find it hard to internalise the difference between profit and cash. It's one of the main reasons companies go out of business.

Here's how I look at it. **Profit** is a number that accountants create to show how much money your business is making. It is both **theoretical and subjective**. People can have different opinions about just how profitable their company actually is, and there are different ways of measuring it, too.

Cash, on the other hand, is **real and objective**. It's the money you have in your bank at any one time... You can always put a figure on it.

The problems start when you confuse the two. As a business owner, you might see lots of money in your account and think it's all there to spend.

But lots of cash in the bank doesn't mean you have any profit. You might have a lot of obligations coming down the line: tax, NI, wages, rent and so on. If you've already spent that money you won't be able to meet those liabilities, and the very viability of your business will be threatened. Your cash doesn't become profit until you've covered all your overheads.

For a long while, it might not be clear how profitable you are, if at all – ask all the businesses I've come across who have had to sue to get money owed to them. And that really is the key – to understand how much money you're actually making, you need to take the long view.

You need to understand not just what's in your account and on your balance sheet today, but what's going to happen tomorrow as well: which bills are coming in, which payments are going to materialise, and how much money you're really going to be left with a few months down the line.

To achieve that understanding, you need excellent management accounts, which look forward as well as back.

4. Know where the profit lies in your business

Knowing this accurately is the key to sustainable growth – and it's surprising how many business owners are genuinely shocked when they drill down and find out the answers.

Have you ever heard of the Pareto Principle? It's the theory that **20%** of your effort generates **80%** of results.

So, for example, **20%** of your salespeople are responsible for **80%** of sales. **20%** of your business's branches bring in **80%** of your revenue. And **20%** of customers generate **80%** of your turnover, too.

Well, obviously it's not always exactly **80/20**. But there's often a scary and actually slightly depressing imbalance between the small areas of your business that create lots of value – and the majority of things you and your staff do every day, which matter a lot less to the bottom line.

Why is this so important?

In order for your business to really prosper, you need to work out which of your products or services are the most profitable. Then you can concentrate on the profit-making side of the business, and either optimise those that are paying the bills, or drop the products and services which are dragging your business down.

Eliminate the soft underbelly of your business and you can really focus on what matters: profit.

But that's actually only the beginning of the story. If you really want to understand where the profit lies in your business, you need to apply the same approach to every area. Analyse which suppliers allow you to operate at the highest profit margins... And which may actually be costing you money.

Examine which members of staff are generating the most value for you... And which are sitting at their desks surfing the Internet, doing nothing!

You need to look at the way you spend your own time

How much of your day are you spending on activities that are pushing your business forward, for example formulating a business strategy, finding new business and – of course – ensuring that your cash flow is running smoothly? And how much time do you spend bogged down in **£10**/hour work that could be performed by somebody else?

Once you've established underperforming areas, you can decide whether there's room for improvement, or whether you should eliminate them altogether. Your goal should be to maximise what's profitable and minimise what isn't. Therein lies the road to riches.

The importance of taking a firm grasp of this aspect of your business cannot be overstated. If you know which of your products and services is delivering profit – not just generating income – you can focus on them.

Then take your loss-making projects, and either work to make them more profitable; or, if that's not possible, drop them. You'll be making more money immediately.

Don't just work out where your profit lies and then assume that this will always apply. Business conditions change all the time, so conduct this exercise regularly.

Your white widgets might have been your most profitable item last year – that doesn't mean they are this year, if the cost of your raw materials or staff has crept up.

And keep your eye on the prize. Would you rather run a **£1 million** company that was profitable, or a **£5 million** company that was not?

To really grow, you need to focus on profit, not on turnover.

5. Why cash flow is king, or... Ten great credit control tips to help you improve your cash flow

You've heard of *Bank of Mum and Dad...* but what about the cash machine of customer credit?

When you give credit to customers, giving them an extended period of time to pay invoices, you're giving them an interest-free loan with no security and no guarantee that you will be paid. Show me a bank that will do that!

Now in your customer's eyes, that may make you look like a really nice guy. But the reality is, you're funding THEIR business at the very considerable risk to your own.

Let me explain in three easy stages.

1. Cash flow. This is the momentum to your business – it's like the oil in the machine. If the cash is in your customer's account rather than yours, it will constrain your decision making. You won't be able to buy new stock. You won't be able to invest in your business. You won't be able to do the things you need to do.

2. Reputation. If you're not getting paid by your customers, you may not be able to pay your suppliers. That's going to affect your credit score and might affect your ability to buy new product too.

3. Risk. This one's easy. What happens to your business if your customer never gets round to paying?

So how do we improve our cash flow?

First, you need to get a grip on the typical cash cycle in your company: understanding the cash cycle is vital to predicting the cash flow in your business – and how much cash it needs to keep it running smoothly. This is one element of what we call working capital.

Secondly, it's important to know what may delay your cash cycle – and so hold your business up from replacing stock or settling vital bills. Your cash flow forecast should be at least as long as your cash cycle.

Here are my **ten** top credit management tips

1. The first one, crazy as it might seem, is not to give your customers credit. No, really, you don't have to give them credit. Ask them for payment upfront, or for part-payment upfront. Make sure you get some cash on the table if you possibly can. You'd be surprised how easy it is. The mythical 30 days is just that. Mythical. Think how often you pay for what you buy up front...

2. Whatever payment terms you set, be rigid with them. Make sure your customers know them and stick to them. In the long run it will pay you dividends.

3. Always credit check. Even on your regular customers after you've been trading with them for a while. Things change. Make sure you know what risks you are taking, and how creditworthy they are. Remember you are effectively loaning them your money!

4. Raise your invoices promptly – perhaps even on the day you make your sale. It's amazing how many people leave it for weeks before they send an invoice out. Get your invoice in as soon as it's realistically do-able and you'll get paid quicker.

5. Deal with queries quickly. Queries are a great way for customers to delay payment. They might even make them up! Get them off the table. When a query comes in sort it out and move on.

6. Make it easy to pay. This one staggers me. How many invoices do you see that show no information about how they should be paid? Put everything on your invoice to make payment easier – bank details, debit/credit card facilities and any other method of payment you can accept – and make it clear what you'd like people to do.

7. Have a systematic approach. It is important with credit control that you have a process-driven way of doing things. Do everything on time, and keep detailed notes of any interactions with your customers so you know what was said, by whom, and when.

8. Send statements. Most people think these are old fashioned and not needed any more. But sending a statement to your customers once a month is a great way of reminding them of you, and what they owe you, and also ensuring that they haven't missed any of your invoices.

9. Being personal is best. It's all well and good having automated systems to send letters and emails, but the personal touch can often yield great results. A handwritten note, a personalised email or even a call can make a big difference to your business.

10. Finally, number ten: don't be afraid to lose your customer. At the end of the day, it's your money and you need to collect it. If you have to take legal action to do that, so be it.

Remember, a sale is not a sale until the money is in YOUR bank. So when it comes to customer credit... no more Mr Nice Guy!

6. Make use of the hidden cash in your business

All businesses need money to invest and grow, but finding it can often be tricky.

So if you're looking for money to support your growth, you might employ the business equivalent of searching down the back of the sofa. Yes, there are lots of places inside every company where money can be released... if you know where to look.

Take the example of a client of mine – let's call him Brian. His company was at a critical phase. He was taking on so many new customers that he needed to hire more staff and buy new equipment. And yet, money was still tight.

The banks were unwilling to lend him more money. Yet with a little bit of hard work he managed to come up with **thousands** of pounds – all of it interest-free.

How did Brian do it? Well, he realised a simple truth. The money he needed was right under his nose, locked up in his own business.

Look at your own business. Where might hidden cash be lurking?

1. Do you have any property which is unused? Brian realised he had a lot of spare office space, so he started renting it out – giving himself a much needed source of additional income.

2. Can you re-sell any old equipment? Brian paid for part of his much-needed IT systems upgrade by selling off his old equipment.

3. Do you have any old stock which has not been sold or is moving slowly? Why not sell this at cost? It will free up some much-needed funds.

4. Get in touch with any debtors who are slow to pay. Most companies have these – it's one of the leading causes of small business failure. So chase late payments more effectively. You could encourage customers to pay up more quickly by incentivising prompt payment plans: a discount for fast settlement.

5. Speak to your suppliers and try to negotiate more favourable payment terms. If you are a regular customer, they may well be willing to give you more time – allowing you to do more with the money. As long as they trust the money is coming in at some point – and it doesn't impact their own cash-flow too much – they will probably be willing to offer some flexibility.

6. Shopping around can also be surprisingly lucrative. Many businesses are paying well over the odds for basic bills such as energy and business insurance. Don't accept the price your existing suppliers are offering – there's almost certainly a better deal elsewhere.

7. Kill waste. Every business has it. Examine all your processes and make certain they are as efficient as possible. If you can make multiple small savings across the scope of your business they will add up in time to something quite significant.

8. A more effective pricing structure can also unlock more profits. Businesses in the UK miss out on millions of pounds' worth of extra profits because their products and services are priced too low. Work out if there's any wriggle room and if you could get away with charging a little more here and there.

Almost every business has money to be found somewhere. Examining yours can not only unearth some of these hidden cash pockets, but could help you refine your future operations.

7. Don't run out of cash!

Running out of cash is the number one reason why businesses fail. So don't let it happen to you.

In fact, being profitable can actually be dangerous. Take Ashley Cooper's business, for instance. It was about to go under. In just a matter of hours, he needed to make a **$270,000** payroll.

There was only one problem: he didn't have the money in the bank. If the staff at his firm, Canada's Paladin Security, all cashed their pay cheques (this was in the mid-1990s), the business would be so overdrawn it would have to close.

There was no one to lend him the money. He lay awake all night, certain he was about to lose everything. Luckily, this story has a happy – and somewhat miraculous – ending.

That very day, several clients paid their overdue bills. Cooper quite literally ran to the bank, and was able to pay his staff. "It was our biggest deposit ever at that time," he told *The Globe and Mail* newspaper **20** years later. "Sometimes there's a great white light that shines on people."

Happy ending. But how did Cooper get into so much trouble? Simple.

His business had been growing so fast, and was so profitable, that he just assumed he didn't have to worry about money. Paladin invoiced late, didn't follow up on overdue payments and paid all its own bills on time, whether or not they had the cash. When its customers' cheques failed to materialise, the company nearly closed: an important lesson for every business owner.

Lots of sales do not necessarily mean that you have money in the bank.

It's really easy to get complacent if you're profitable. But some of your clients may regularly take **60** days to pay you. And you always risk dealing with customers who either cannot or will not pay. If, in the meanwhile, a big VAT bill arrives or a customer defaults, it's game over.

As CEO, you need to be constantly aware of how much money is moving in and out of your company. Make sure you know when customers are due to pay you, when you're expected to pay bills and when there might be a gap between the two. That way, if you forecast a shortfall you can act to avoid catastrophe, by negotiating more favourable payment terms with your suppliers or shifting payment dates, for example.

Remember: running out of cash is the number **one** reason why businesses fail.

So just what can you do to head off this problem at the pass? In essence, you are trying to close the gap between payments coming in and payments going out. Here are **five** top tips to help you stay in the black:

1. Look at your cash flow statements on a weekly, if not daily, basis to ensure your customers are sticking to your terms. If you're not comfortable with spreadsheets, make sure that you ask your finance team for regular cash flow reports that are easy for you to understand.

2. Go to any customers paying over the 30 days mark and see if they can pay quicker. You could offer a discount or simply renegotiate the terms.

3. Negotiate a better deal with your suppliers that will help close the gap.

4. Alternatively, ask your suppliers for consignment stock. That way you pay for the stock when you sell it, not when you receive it from them.

5. If you are still faced with problems, maybe it's time to examine the whole way your business is financed. Perhaps you've reached the stage where you need to introduce some funding.

8. When should you raise your prices?

One of the toughest decisions any business makes is timing its price increases. You only have to look at the furore faced by the makers of Marmite when they tried to push up the prices being paid by the big supermarkets to realise that – after years of low inflation in this country – no one accepts increases lightly.

But after years of supply line efficiencies stemming the inflationary tide, we are now facing a global economy where most of the fat has been stripped of the bone. As developing nations look to raise living standards, prices will start to edge up. Currency fluctuations can make anything containing imported components more expensive.

Small companies who continue to keep taking the hits will reach the point where they are simply trading, not making a profit – which is unsustainable. What do the big companies do in these circumstances? Here is an interesting (and true) tale...

2015 looked like a tough year for Coca Cola. Health-conscious consumers were turning away from fizzy drinks. Add to that the downturn in the dollar, and it seemed likely that the company would take a painful hit.

So what did they do? They raised prices in North America by **4%**. The result? Within **six** months, a **20%** rise in profits.

Now, I know what you're probably thinking. "That's all right for Coca Cola. They can do whatever they want – people are addicted to their products! If we raised our prices, sales would drop. If we want more business, it would be better to cut prices – not raise them."

Luckily, that's not true. In almost all cases, the number one thing you can do to increase profits is to put your prices up. Unlike other methods of increasing profits – cutting costs, selling more – it can be done quickly, and the results are immediate.

It's important to remember that even very small price increases can result in large changes to your profitability (as in the Coca Cola example). How so? I don't want to get bogged down in figures here, but think of it this way.

Imagine you're selling a product for **£100**, which costs you **£80** to bring to market. Your profit is **£20**. Increase your price to **£105**, and your profit margin per item will rise to **£25**. So, for a small price increase of **5%**, your profits have grown by **25%**.

You don't even have to raise your prices by that much. According to research by McKinsey, even a **1%** hike in prices can raise your profits by **11%**.

Nor do you have to increase your prices across the board. If, for example, you know which of your products or services are least profitable, you can restrict your price rises to them only. Or you could work out which clients are getting the best deals from you, and start charging them more.

The fear, of course, is that if you raise your prices, you will lose some of your customers. And you're right. That might happen. But because you're charging more, you can afford to lose some sales; you will probably still make more money than before.

If you're really lucky, you will even get rid of your problem customers, those who are squeezing you for every penny instead of making you richer.

Here's another secret: if you offer stellar service, your best customers won't mind if you charge them a little more. They'll probably just wonder what took you so long!

9. Manage your bank – don't let it manage you

Business owners often complain about their relationship with their bank. It's almost always the same issues:

1. "No one's available to answer questions..."
2. "My bank manager show no interest in my business..."
3. "When I need help urgently, they're just not responsive..."

But instead of complaining, why not pick up the phone and talk to them? If you want a relationship with your bank manager, you can't rely on them to do all the heavy lifting. You need to work at it, too.

Make your bank manager your best friend. Don't keep them in the dark — let them know what's going on with your business on a regular basis. Give them good news as well as bad, and send them your monthly management accounts. Invite them for meetings and to visit your company. They'll usually come.

Remember this: they hate surprises, so if you think you're about to hit a bad patch and need their support, get in touch sooner rather than later. They'll be more inclined to help if they can see that you have a long-term plan for your business. It's in their interests to lend you cash, so help them help you.

Size could be an issue, of course. Most banks will not have dedicated relationship managers for small-sized companies, but what they consider 'small' varies. Generally, the lower limit is a turnover of **£1-£2 million**. Some, such as Metro Bank, have no lower limit and will be happy to help you out no matter what the size of your business.

Many people consider their bank manager their enemy, but they don't have to be. They can be your biggest friend and supporter, giving you great advice, helping you tide over difficult periods and smoothing out issues quickly. So don't leave it to your bank manager to reach out first... the relationship is far too important for you to leave it to them!

But what if you are with the wrong bank?

All that said... If you've encountered the problems I discussed at the beginning of this chapter and made every effort to make the relationship work, then it may be time to recalibrate. If your bank is unwilling to enter into a meaningful (and helpful) relationship then they are actually holding your business back.

Not being able to speak directly is a key issue – especially for smaller businesses. All too often contact involves enduring endless jingles while you get patched through to a call centre, eventually reaching someone who has no authority to make decisions anyway.

Equally, the 'computer says no' syndrome is another cause for complaint – with no regard seemingly taken for a company's trading record. If this sounds like you, consider moving your bank: it's not as difficult as it might sound – even though very few of us ever go through with it!

Indeed, research shows that customers are likely to stick with the same bank once they've opened an account, no matter what. And when they start a business they will almost certainly go to the bank where they have their personal account – even if that bank is not geared up to handle business accounts.

It doesn't make any sense. You should be shopping around for the bank that's best for your company... not just now but in to the future as your business expands.

Not long ago, it didn't matter as much. The four big banks probably all had a branch near you, and offered broadly equivalent services. But following the banking crisis, the industry has gone through a period of enormous change. Not only have the big banks started to break up – welcome, TSB - we've also seen the arrival of new 'challenger' banks such as Metro Bank, Atom, Aldermore, Handelsbanken and others, which are much more niche.

At the same time, many larger banks are closing smaller local branches, with a few abandoning the high street altogether in favour of digital space. There are now genuine differences between the banks... and genuine choice.

Here are **five** factors to consider if you look to move bank:

1. What facilities do you need? Will you frequently be cashing cheques, or depositing large sums of cash? Do you need a deposit box or night safe? If so, you'll need a bank with a physical presence near your HQ. As I said, this is no longer a given for many banks – and over the next decade, high street branches will become even rarer.

2. Internet banking. Banks are doing more and more of their business online. If this is a facility you intend to use often, you must know that their security measures are up to scratch, and their system will do everything you need of it. Consider factors such as approval limits, dual authorisation and the functionality that is available.

3. Foreign payments. Do you conduct businesses overseas? If so, what are the fees like for foreign payments into and out of your account, and how straightforward is it for overseas customers to use? This area is becoming much more competitive.

4. Charges. Exactly how much does the bank charge and what for? Read all the small print and make sure you understand all the charges because banks can be slippery about this. Attractive introductory offers can soon end, leaving you with high monthly charges.

5. What kind of relationship do you want? Do you expect to have a relationship with your bank manager, for example? Depending on your size, not every bank will be able to offer this. Will that relationship change if your business expands above a certain level?

The good news is that moving banks is no longer complicated. Banks will automatically transfer all your standing orders and forward all direct debits made out to you, so there's very little for you to do.

So ask yourself: is your bank really fulfilling your company's needs or is it holding you back? It might just be time to shop around...

10. Manage your borrowing

You've hit a glitch and you're unsure how you're going to get through the next few months... you talk to the bank and their solution is a loan. Perhaps over a couple of years. You could roll up your current overdraft and, they tell you, the interest rates are very reasonable too... yes there's a charge, but there's a charge for extending your overdraft too... just sign here.

It's a common enough tale – enacted **thousands** of times every day.

And, in many circumstances, it is the right solution. But a bank loan is something that every business owner should think about very carefully.

Yes, a loan provides much needed capital, but it also comes with risk and cost.

There's the chance you might struggle to make repayments, and land your business in serious trouble. Interest rates can be a drag on your business when the money does come in; your loan can end up being very expensive.

The reality is that loans have weakened, or even destroyed, many a business – you should think long and hard before you take one.

So in what scenarios should you apply for a bank loan? And when might you be granted one?

Here are **three** key considerations:

1. Are your needs short- or long-term? Do you need the money for something which will have a long-term impact on your business – namely something which can help it grow and thrive? If so, a loan might well be a good idea. However, if you only need it for the next few months to cover a short-term gap, it's not worth the risk, nor will you want to pay the interest over the long-term. You'd be better off with an overdraft.

The rule of thumb is: get long-term funding for long-term needs, and short-term funding for short-term needs. An overdraft is short-term funding as it is repayable on demand and totally flexible.

2. Are the costs justified? Always make a business case for a loan. The first person you must convince is yourself. You need to prove that you have a really good reason for taking on so much risk and paying so much interest.

Say you're investing in equipment. Is the benefit it will give your business enough to justify the expense? If you can make the case to yourself, you'll have a better chance of making the case to a lender – and a better chance of getting a more favourable deal.

3. What if the worst happens? You know the old saying: "Plan for the worst, hope for the best.". What happens if – for some reason – you can't pay it back? You'll be asked for security or collateral – think about whether what you're putting on the line is something you can afford to lose.

Sometimes the lender will ask for the equipment you're buying, but some people will make a personal guarantee against another asset – such as their home. Think long and hard before you do this. I am staggered at how many business owners I have had conversations with, when their business is on its knees, do not know or understand their exposure to personal guarantees!

Luckily, there are alternative sources of finance. Here are **five** other borrowing options you should consider, before taking out a bank loan:

1. Finance Lease or Hire Purchase: Do you need money to buy equipment? If so, a hire purchase arrangement might be the best option. This is, of course, a type of loan, but you're borrowing the money from the company which sells you the equipment or a specialist provider, rather than the bank. Your loan is tied to a specific product.

The downside is that this can be more expensive over the longer term than buying what you need outright, but there's less immediate impact on your cash flow.

2. Operating lease: This is a slight twist on leasing. At the end of the deal you give the equipment back. This is a good idea if you only want it for a short time, or it's the kind of equipment which goes out of date quickly, such as IT. You can then organise a new operating lease agreement – it's a cost-effective way to always have latest technology available. It is in effect a long-term rental.

With these deals you should always read the small print carefully. What happens if your circumstances change? Do you have any flexibility to get out of the lease agreement? Never assume things will be all right – being stuck in an inflexible arrangement can be difficult. Also check who is liable for maintenance and what obligations there are when goods are returned.

Also, be wary of what I call the insurance cheat. These types of agreement place a perfectly reasonable obligation on you to fully insure the asset. Fair enough. What they don't tell you is that, tucked away in the small print, is a clause that says if you do not advise them about the insurance arrangements you have made in a short period of time they will insure it themselves and charge you. This charge then appears as an additional cost on the rentals you are paying, which often goes undetected in the monthly direct debit. They can (and do) just put it up without telling you – and often by an extortionate amount!

3. Peer-to-peer lending: If the banks aren't willing to lend, perhaps the crowd might do it. Peer-to-peer lending is growing, with companies such as Crowd Cube offering private individuals the chance to give loans to businesses.

Each business is given a credit rating based on the level of risk. This can be more affordable, but as with regular business loans, you will still have to make interest payments. Crowd funders are particularly keen on investing money in businesses which will be using the extra funds to introduce new products, or move into new markets.

4. Lending the money yourself: You might be in a position to invest your own cash in the business. If you decide to do this, you need to protect yourself in case things go wrong. Set up the loan in much the same way as you would any other loan – that means taking security, arranging interest and a payment plan, just as any other lenders would do. This protects your position if anything does not quite go according to plan!

5. Reach out to friends and family: Someone in your immediate circle might also be willing to help out with a loan. Again, set this up with all the professionalism and due process you would any other form of loan. You need to protect them too.

All these have their pros and cons – the decision depends on the exact circumstances of your business. And also don't forget the option we discussed earlier: find the cash hidden within your company (every company has some!).

11. Balance the books between months of feast and famine

"Our profit goes up and down like a yo-yo. One month we're doing really well, the next month is a disaster." I initially assumed that

this new client worked with really tight margins and the costs of their raw materials fluctuated, or that perhaps they suffered from currency fluctuations. But it turned out to be something much more prosaic: an accounting mistake.

They paid their office rent on a quarterly basis – and so once every **three** months, it looked like their expenses were out of control, eating into their profits.

This led the owner to some very bad decisions. While he always had the money to pay the rent, he was under the impression that his business was unstable, and was therefore reluctant to invest in areas that needed development. But his business wasn't unstable at all. The rent covered an entire quarter – and so instead of being lumped as one massive expense in his accounts once every **three** months, it should have been spread over **three** months.

It's basic accounting, and yet I can't tell you how many businesses make this type of error, skewing their figures and giving business owners a false sense of their financial position. Unfortunately, many are not aware this is happening.

Put yourself in the shoes of a gym owner. Every January he has a spurt of new members eager to work off Christmas excesses. He offers a discount to people who pay upfront for the year, leading to a flood of cash. He feels pretty good about life!

Let's hope he doesn't splurge too much... Because those people weren't just paying for January – they were paying for an entire year. Over the next **12** months, the gym owner will have to use all that money to pay for the equipment, staff and his own rent – leading to an entirely different financial picture... Possibly even a loss.

Even worse, some of that money which seemed like a sure thing in January can disappear overnight. **Six** months down the line, many of those January sign-ups will have decided to quit, and ask for a partial refund.

If this gym owner's accounts in January showed a bonanza month, he might expect a bonanza year as well. And yet that might not be a truthful representation of what was happening in his business. In reality, those payments were meant to cover **12** months – and should be spread out in his accounts, accordingly. This is a far more accurate picture of his finances.

A related issue for many businesses is that you have to enter expenses and revenues when they are incurred, rather than when cash changes hands. So for example, if you send out a long list of invoices in January which don't get paid until April, it is essential that you record these as January sales, not as April sales.

Similarly, if you put in an order for the delivery of raw materials in June, that's when it needs to appear on your accounts – not in August, when you pay for them. And if you know that you're expecting a bill in June and it hasn't arrived, you still must account for it in June – then chase it up!

The key is that you need an accurate representation of your income and expenses in any given period.

Accountant's speak for this is 'accruals and prepayments' but at the end of the day it's just about making your **numbers** meaningful and not misleading.

If you simply record when the cash comes in and out, you'll get a distorted picture – and we all know what that leads to: bad business decisions.

12. The danger of direct debits

Several years ago, a regional UK newspaper that had suffered a sharp drop in readership undertook a complete financial review.

To the management's horror, they discovered that they had been paying several freelancers a monthly retainer, even though they hadn't filed a story in over **30** years! Yet in **three** decades, no one had noticed.

As this horror story shows, putting payments on autopilot is a double-edged sword. On the one hand, it simplifies your expenses. But on the other hand, when not managed properly, it can cause an incredible waste of money and contribute to serious cash flow problems.

As your business grows, you may well set up various forms of payments through direct debits – everything from rent, utilities and insurance to trade paper subscriptions and so on.

These direct debits might have been set up by various people at different times, so it's not uncommon for a business to be uncertain about exactly what it is paying out.

Even worse, even if the payments are warranted, what seemed like a good deal several years ago may be expensive now. But with direct debits, payments can continue for years before anyone reviews the price you're paying.

The biggest obstacle to getting these payments under control is simple inertia – "we've always done it this way". But if you are looking to grow your business, it's important to manage your accounts more proactively.

Start by regularly auditing all your direct debits.

1. Draw up a comprehensive list of what's going out and what on.
2. Always ask yourself whether this is something you still need in your business. In many cases it's an expenditure which was important in your early days, but has become much less relevant over time.
3. Once you've sorted out the waste, look at your direct debits and see if you can get these products or services cheaper another way. Many businesses stick with the same supplier for things such as utilities, but if you spend a little time browsing the market, you might be able to get a better deal elsewhere.

These savings may be small on their own, but like the expenses, they can add up pretty quickly.

If you find yourself wading through a huge amount of outdated direct debits, it is a sign that your accounts are in pretty bad shape. Your business will find it hard to grow to its full potential and make maximum profit if your expenses are shrouded in mystery – and if you are regularly overpaying for products and services.

So make this (at the very least!) an annual exercise.

13. Control your expenses

One business owner was shocked to discover that staff expenses had doubled over **24** months. The CEO, who was very trusting (some might say naïve) did not oversee expenses, and it wasn't until a new office manager queried why staff expenses were so high that the scale of the problem truly hit home.

It turned out that key members of staff had access to a company credit card. Since there were no written guidelines about what they could claim, employees took a broad view, for example, charging for a weekly meal for the sales team. As nothing was ever challenged, no one ever thought twice about it... until expenses ballooned out of control!

It's human nature; if we're given access to a company credit card, we're likely to be much less careful than if we have to spend our own money.

So how can you keep a tight lid on expenses? The key is to lay down firm ground rules about what staff are allowed to claim, by writing a company expenses policy. Most are honest and will stay within the guidelines they are given.

Where possible (and practical), avoid giving staff access to a company credit card. It is much harder to reject expenses once they've already been charged to the card.

A much better approach is to make staff pay expenses from their own pocket and claim them back with an expenses request. Not only are people naturally more careful when the money initially comes out of their own account, but it will also be easier for you to refuse payments that seem excessive or unwarranted.

Whether staff are charging expenses to a company card or claiming back later, review claims at least once a month. Regular reviews will make your team much more conscious of what they're charging to the company. It will also make it easier for you to see if you're spending more than absolutely necessary.

You want to charge WHAT to your business?!

Of course, it's not just staff who can sometimes extract the metaphorical when it comes to expenses. I've had a number of clients – the business owners themselves – who have been guilty of the same offence.

Over the years, I've seen it all, from people charging their mortgage to their business (who were flabbergasted when I told them it was taxable income) to one client who put their au pair on the payroll. It took some time to work out because the name was just one among many employees, but I got there in the end.

Many business owners dip into business funds in order to pay for personal things. And that can be dangerous. **One**, you are distorting the true performance of the company, making it very difficult to adhere to meaningful budgets. **Two**, HMRC hates this behaviour because it's an attempt to get money tax-free. Yes, there will be moments when you find you've got the wrong card on you. But if you decide to pay for personal items through the business you have **two** choices: pay money back really quickly or be prepared to pay tax on it.

Others make an honest mistake. The rules can be complex, and people are not always aware of some of the finer points.

But that's your responsibility. You need to be clear about the rules – and if you're not then you need to check. And most important of all, don't push your luck and hope HMRC fails to notice.

Even within the past **two** years, they are taking this much more seriously. If they discover you have been taking money out of the business for personal purposes, they can charge penalties and levy punitive interest.

Even if they don't notice, don't do it. Taking money out of the business to fund personal expenses is a terrible and unprofessional way to run your company. You are depriving it of funds it needs to function, thrive and grow, as well as being fundamentally dishonest to yourself. Is that any way to build a proper business?

Even if you've founded the company and consider it yours, look at it as an entirely separate entity – not an extension of your personal world... that is not what it is. Your neighbour has no responsibility to pay your mortgage or shell out for your Christmas presents – neither does your business! Your business might well have other shareholders: at the very least you are short-changing them.

There are areas where the lines might blur, but stick to this general rule of thumb: if you didn't have the business, would you have paid that expense anyway? If the answer is yes – for example, you would have met that friend for coffee regardless – don't charge it.

Ultimately, of course, claim for what you rightfully can. You should never be out of pocket for expenses that are genuinely business-related. So, if you travelled by car to a business meeting, claim that mileage even if it was only a little. It all adds up.

But make sure you are honest and transparent about what you're charging to the business, and keep good records. It'll save you a lot of hassle in the long run.

14. Manage your credit rating

When someone's looking to work with you, they will most likely check your company out on your website, and your social media outlets. They might also visit LinkedIn, to look into the individual backgrounds of you and your fellow directors.

And, not least, they'll more than likely check your credit rating to see if you're a solid, reliable company on a sound financial footing. If it's a potential supplier looking you up, they want to make sure you can pay your bills. Yet many companies never spare their own credit report a second thought.

So when was the last time you checked yours? It's worth doing, and doing so regularly, because sadly, sometimes the credit agencies get things wrong.

I have a client in a great financial position, but one year when they filed their accounts at Companies House a leading credit agency (which shall not be named) misinterpreted them. Their credit rating was immediately downgraded, making it look as if they were in serious financial trouble.

The fact that it was wrong was besides the point. Once it's online, potential clients – and others – will draw their own conclusions. Your reputation and important relationships can be damaged. Business can be lost.

This really isn't that uncommon. Another client of ours based in the UK had the same name as a company in Ireland. The credit agency got them mixed up, and as a result their accounts looked much worse than they really were. Luckily, I picked up both cases because I monitor clients' credit ratings. And that's something you need to do for your company too.

If there is a mistake, get in contact with the credit agency quickly to tell them about the error. Their business depends on them having the right information so they will generally be happy to help out. It's in their interest to do just that, as their credibility depends on it.

And it's in your interests to make sure that you are represented accurately, wherever you are online.

Equally, if your credit report is genuinely poor, then it's potentially a challenge to the way you run your business. Suppliers can get difficult and demand better terms. If you go for credit, it's likely to be more expensive. Even potential customers may reject you because you represent a risk to their supply chain.

There **ARE** ways to improve your credit ratings.

Here are **five** very handy ones:

1. What's on your record?
Check what negatives are counting against you and see if these can be improved or removed.

2. Ensure any old County Court Judgements have been struck off
CCJs are bad news on a credit check, so if you have had one against you at any time, and you've cleared it, do make sure that your record is up to date. Unpaid CCJs will appear on the register for up to **six** years. A letter of confirmation from the individual or

company which filed the judgment may be needed in order to receive a certificate of satisfaction or cancellation, and should be presented to the County Court.

3. Keep your personal finances in good order

Anyone considering offering you credit may also check your own track record – especially if your business does not have a long trading history.

4. Applying for credit can count against you

Remember that each time you apply for a loan, it is registered and can be viewed as a negative factor – even if the application isn't turned down.

5. Keep your company records up to date

A first port of call for many people looking at your track record will be Companies House. If you are late with filing your returns, it may well count against you.

In fact credit agencies will downgrade your rating the nearer you get to the filing deadline. They take the view that if it takes you that long to get your accounts filed then either you are hiding something, or you are in such a mess that you cannot produce them. Neither is a particularly good reflection on your business.

So here's your mission for the next few minutes. Google your company name, and 'credit report'. See what it throws up... and ask yourself: would you be happy for potential clients to view the same results?

15. Do you really need that new employee?

Business is booming. Your staff are struggling to keep up. But before you make that new hire, think carefully. Can you really afford it? And is there a better solution?

Very often, companies underestimate how much a new employee is really going to cost them. Beyond the headline salary (together with National Insurance, pension obligations and payroll administration) you've got to add in all the recruitment costs – the advertising and agency fees, as well as the time invested by you and/or others in the company.

Then you have to supply IT equipment, desk space, and a string of benefits, which can run from free coffee to private healthcare.

There are hidden costs to absorbing that new worker, too. Every new member of your staff needs to be inducted and trained. It's estimated that it takes an average of **23** weeks before an employee gets up to full speed – and much longer for more complex roles.

And remember, you still have to pay this person when they're not being productive – enjoying their holiday entitlement, at home sick, or wasting time at work (let's face it, even people who own their own business waste some time at work – or at least I do!).

Plus of course, you still have to pay them when you're having a slack month. In fact, with no compulsory retirement age, I think of taking on a staff member as a lifetime commitment. What will that **30**-year-old employee cost over time?

And let's even not start on the risks to your business if you hire the wrong person...

Now, this doesn't mean that hiring is always the wrong decision – clearly that's not the case! But before you start the search process, I suggest you examine whether your procedures can be improved first to remove the need for the additional expenditure you're about to incur.

When a business is growing fast, it is often wedded to ways of working which may have been adequate when it was smaller – but are completely inefficient when it expands. Even the introduction of a more efficient software programme can enable you to run leaner... so do check out all your options before going down the employment route.

Take time to thoroughly review how you are operating, how your people are spending their time, where there is duplication and time wasting, room for error and additional costs. Then, possibly, invest in new systems, new practices and new ways of working before you go down the route of investing in more people.

Often the investment in something like a new computerised system that can replace an outmoded manual process can pay huge dividends. And remember, computer systems don't take holidays, don't go sick (well, OK, maybe sometimes!), are more robust and often much more reliable than another human!

SECTION 3: Valuing your future

> " The **bad news** is time flies.
> The **good news** is you're the pilot. "

Altshuler

Presumably you don't want to work for ever... so what does the pot of gold at the end of YOUR rainbow look like?

Whether it's retiring to the golf course in time to acquire a respectable handicap, gradually reducing your work commitments in the years ahead, selling to the highest possible bidder or cementing your family's future by passing on the reins of a successful business, you will need to have certain things in place.

This last section takes you through the principal areas you need to build into your plans. Not least, reading this will help you avoid the potential hazards that will make it impossible to sell... let alone achieve its true market value.

1. Define your long-term objective

> " The **starting** point of all achievement
> is desire. Keep this **constantly** in mind.
> Weak desires bring **weak results**, just
> as a small amount of fire makes
> a small amount of heat. "
>
> Napoleon Hill

Thinking ahead several years, what's your long-term plan for your business?

I ask this because, for some reading this book, the monetary value of their business will matter to them. Not just those looking to sell their enterprise at some point in the future, but also anyone who might look for external investment, or perhaps raise finance through borrowing, or use their business as a form of security.

Just knowing you have built up a business worth a lot of money can be a nice feeling in itself!

For others the value is less important than other factors. Many are happy owning a lifestyle business. Their main priorities are generating a comfortable income and having flexibility and control over their time. They're not really interested in growing their company aggressively or maximising its value.

There will be those who see themselves passing it on to family members when they eventually retire. That means they want to make sure it's on a sound footing, and bring their family on board when it's right to do so.

But for those who plan to sell up some time down the line, and want to build up their business to the point where it is an attractive purchase, focusing on its value gives them a goal: a point at which they can either retire happily on the proceeds, or start the entire exercise again with another company.

If you think that is even a vague possibility, you need to start planning now – **and this section is just for you!**

Even if you're not yet ready for a detailed exit plan, indeed, even if you are only in the foothills of where you want to take your enterprise, it's never too early to conjure up a clear idea about where your business will be when it is complete (the point in time when, maybe, you are ready to sell).

With that vision in mind, you can systematically build your company in the correct way, so that when the time is right, you can exit — easily and for the maximum price.

Most companies grow 'organically'. They start off small, take on new people, open new branches perhaps, increase their production or sales capacity... and regularly find themselves having to adjust the way the business is run.

And while that works for many people, it does not (as earlier sections of this book explain) make for a smooth passage for growth: you're constantly banging your head against the brick wall of self-imposed restrictions.

Equally, if you allow your company to develop more organically, you may find that it is not attractive to a buyer when you decide it's time to sell up, and that you have several years of work to do to make it fit for sale.

Life may well get in the way of your plans and unforeseen opportunities or challenges might take you in a completely differently direction — no one can predict the future, and this isn't about being rigid in your approach. But as with everything in business, you should begin with an end in mind.

2. Start with the end in mind

> 66 If you **don't know** where you are going, any road will get you there. 99

Lewis Carroll

So right from the beginning, visualise what your business will look like when you sell it.

1. **How big will it be?**
2. **How many locations will it have?**
3. **What management structure will be in place?**
4. **How much money will it be making?**

Bearing all that in mind, what might be your target price? That could well be the amount of money you calculate you need to retire comfortably, or to invest in your next venture. An end figure like that might give you a target to aim for.

To that end, you will also need to put yourself in the position of your target buyer. When you do come to approach an agent to sell your business, the first question will be: Who might buy it – and why?

And that's the most important part of your vision: to build a company that is attractive to potential buyers. A business they can take over and run from Day **One** with no input from you. An enterprise that relies on systems, not people. An asset which retains its customers and key members of staff when you walk out the door for the last time.

That makes the section on systematising your business critical. Why not take a look back at page 74 to remind yourself!

Gerber says that you should try to build a business that you could franchise and replicate. It doesn't matter whether you have any interest in franchising per se, it's simply a way to help you focus on creating a venture which isn't dependent on any individual. Instead, you put in place systems and processes which anyone can use and execute.

3. Identify prospective purchasers

66 The **wonderful** thing about **not** planning, is that **failure** comes as a **complete surprise** and is **not** preceded by periods of **stress** and **worry**. 99

Anonymous

There are different categories of people or companies who might, when the time is right, be interested in your business.

1. First of all, there are those already in your sector – probably a competitor who may want to either acquire your market share, take advantage of the technology or patents you have, or perhaps update their own operation harnessing your equipment or distribution network.

2. Then there are passive investors, who want to continue to run your business as it is now. They might want you to manage it for a fixed period while they get their own people installed.

3. There are companies who want to expand, perhaps doing something aligned with you but not competing with you. For instance, if you make plastic widgets, you might be bought by another company in your supply chain – a plastics manufacturer say, or a widget distributor.

4. And, finally, your own management team might be interested in acquiring the business from you: they have the advantage of not only knowing how your business runs, but also being well aware of its strengths, weaknesses, future opportunities and challenges. Acquiring the business will also mean they get to keep their jobs!

The way you develop your business might change if you know you're aiming to sell to a competitor, as opposed to one of your current suppliers, because their respective needs will be different. Equally, if you have discussed a future management buy-out with your team then it needs to be talked through and planned over a sufficient amount of time to make the transition smooth, and for independent assessments on the value of the business to be made that will be fair to both sides.

In my business, I get involved in any **number** of exit plans, as well as the sales that follow. None of them come out of the blue. All successful sales take place on the back of decisions about the strategic direction of the business which were made long, long before.

One aspect that many people find difficult to come to terms with is that, to sell your business, you need to make yourself irrelevant to it. If you don't, people aren't buying the business – they're buying you. And the last thing they'll want to have to depend on is the person who has just sold them their business.

4. Avoid 'rogue shareholders'

> ❝Train people well enough so they can **leave**, treat them **well enough** so they don't want to.❞
>
> Richard Branson

Several years ago I was involved in a sale which almost fell apart – because the company had **one** shareholder who was against the deal.

He didn't care that he was outnumbered **three**-to-**one**. He saw himself as the responsible **one**, holding out against a short-term deal to make a quick buck. The others had been courting the buyer for some time, working towards a sale for a couple of years. But they'd not really talked to the fourth shareholder about their plans.

Perhaps that wasn't surprising, given that he hadn't been involved in the business for a **number** of years. But it was a mistake.

If you have multiple owners in your business, you really need to know – way ahead – what will happen if shareholders have differing views about selling up.

'Rogue shareholders' can cause huge problems, sometimes by refusing to sell, and at other times by selling to the wrong party – a rival company for example. Or they may just threaten to sell, trying to gain the upper hand in a dispute.

It's essential that you're all covered by a shareholders' agreement – and that you draw one up early on.

A shareholders' agreement is a legally binding contract between the co-owners of a business, outlining how it's run, and also what happens if anyone decides to sell their shares (look at it as a sort of prenuptial agreement!).

It can control when owners are allowed to sell their shares, who can buy them, and what price will be paid. Some shareholders' agreements will state that shares can only be sold when an owner retires, goes bankrupt, becomes disabled, gets divorced, or dies.

Others allow more freedom – but still lay down clear procedures to follow.

For example, another company I work with has **two** owners, one of whom has decided to retire early, in his **50s**, and sell his share of the business. Because they have a shareholder's agreement, there is already a defined path to let that happen smoothly.

All the owners of a business want to profit from it. But if you don't think about exits right from the beginning, disputes could well severely damage the very asset you all need to build.

5. No one will buy your company without this...

> " Luck is what happens when **preparation** meets opportunity. "

Darrell Royal

Several years ago I was helping with the sale of a business, which involved a very lengthy due diligence process.

Why did it take so long? Because the accountants were desperate to find evidence of any financial weakness they could use to push the price down.

They spent weeks examining every financial record in detail, but they couldn't uncover any ammunition at all.

Eventually the sale went through at the full price, and the buyer asked me to stay on – "to keep up the good work" – as my company was responsible for managing this company's accounts. In short, there was nothing in the books that looked dodgy, every payment was accounted for and there were no skeletons to be uncovered by someone who knows where to look.

I'm not mentioning this just because it's nice to recount success stories. No, it's really because I want to talk about the importance of good governance if you ever want to sell your business. This is no quick-fix solution just before a sale, but more of a long-term investment you need to make years before.

When I decided to sell my last car, I made sure it had a good deep clean to get it ready. But much more important was the full service history from a main dealer, and the annual MOT certificates showing that the mileage was genuine and that the car had been roadworthy and well-taken care of over several years. It's very similar with a business. But instead of an MOT and service history, you need to show great stewardship and control.

You need to be able to demonstrate you've been running a tight ship, with no sinister financial details lurking in the background. That means no personal assets on the balance sheet. No old unpaid debts. No old stock or machinery that should have been sold off. No funny **numbers** to cover up your true financial position. And absolutely no mistakes in your accounts.

Your records need to prove that whenever a third party has looked into your business, you've come out smelling of roses. So you must be ready at all times for an audit report, or a VAT or PAYE inspection, with full records that are easy to access.

Consistency, or your ability to demonstrate that you have delivered strong results year-on-year, is a very important element of all this. Any buyer will want to think they can continue where you've left off.

Of course, the other thing any buyer will want is a keen price. And if their due diligence throws up anything even remotely suspect, they'll be expecting a reduction – assuming they don't walk away from the deal entirely.

6. So how much IS your business worth?

> "A **bend** in the road is **not** the **end** of the road ... unless you **fail** to make the **turn**."
>
> Unknown

Or, loosely translated: opportunity is what you make of it.

But the point is this: a business (like anything else) is only worth what someone's prepared to pay for it.

There's a specialist group of people who will value a business for a fee. They will look at a whole raft of factors: turnover; gross profit; net profit; market share; brand value; patents and copyrights; the customer/client list; and the expertise of key personnel.

Alongside that, potential buyers will calculate how the acquisition will impact on their own business; can they make economies through using **one** distribution network rather than **two**? Will they be able to charge more for their own product lines if they take yours off the market? Will they be able to tender for contracts for other parts of their business once they have got in the door with your clients?

The list goes on. But if you are looking to sell, rather than the other party seeking you out, and there is only one prospective buyer, you're not in a great place to negotiate a higher price.

But there are some key ways in which you can make yourself attractive – and remove potential obstacles. And these are points already covered in the book, but I shall make the main ones again:

1. Make your business systems dependent, not one reliant on people (especially yourself).

2. Make sure there are no financial skeletons in the cupboard.

3. If more than one person has a say in when or how the business is sold, plan an exit strategy in advance and have a signed shareholders' agreement in place.

Fail to get any of those in place, and a sale won't achieve the value you're hoping for, and it might not happen at all.

10 action points to take away from this book

1. Have a plan. Make sure your understand what your business will look like when it's finished – and how you are going to get there.

2. Put a sign on your desk or your wall saying 'cash is king' and never forget it. Many businesses that fail are actually profitable – but they grow so quickly that they run out of cash.

3. Know and understand the numbers in your business – they're the equivalent of the instruments on your car. If you know what they mean you will make better decisions.

4. Make sure you get detailed management accounts on your desk on a regular and frequent basis – that means monthly. Without these, you're flying blind.

5. Know where the profit lies in your business – it's surprising how many owners are taken aback when they find out the answer, but it's the key to sustainable growth.

6. Grow the value in your business through the systems you put in place. This means a key member of staff could walk away tomorrow, or you could sell the business, and the company would still continue to run smoothly.

7. Set budgets within your business which will push you into creating plans of action to achieve those targets. And remember: a budget is not a financial forecast – it is a plan of action to achieve an outcome. The financial forecast is a separate element which will show you what that outcome will look like. So major on the action first – and the numbers will follow!

8. Business is built on teamwork, so make sure that all of the people that you need to drive the company forward understand your plans for the future – and are made to feel part of that future (this includes stakeholders, such as your bank, and other backers).

9. If you don't know the answer, never be afraid to ask someone who does. And if you don't have an essential skill within your company, buy it in to plug that gap.

10. Finally... persevere! Of all the qualities you need to succeed in business, perseverance is probably key. Look at all the richest people in the world; they have all gone through difficult times, but have been buoyed up by their vision and determination.

Don't be baffled by the jargon!

The accountancy profession, like many others, is really good at using terms and expressions that confuse those who need to read and understand the very stuff they are talking about. This is especially the case when it is your business we are discussing.

So, this glossary is intended to explain each term that commonly comes up in a way that I hope you will understand and that will help you when your accountant or finance director seems to be speaking a different language!

Accruals and prepayments

A fundamental accounting principle which is very important is 'matching'. That is in any given financial period (on which you are reporting) the income and the costs included all relate to that period and therefore match. If this is not done, some pretty large distortions can come into play especially if you are looking at say a month and it includes a significant annual cost.

The way accountants deal with this is through making accruals and prepayments. Accruals are adjustments to add a cost into a period that has perhaps not yet been charged but relates to that period; perhaps a cost where the invoice has not been received. Prepayments are the opposite, moving costs incurred in the period into future periods.

Amortisation

This is another name for depreciation, but is generally used to recognise the reduction in value of intangible assets rather than physical assets. With physical assets it is often possible to make a well informed judgement of how long the asset will last for, however with many intangible assets this is often more difficult.

Assets

Assets are the things the company owns. These might be long term physical items like plant, machinery, buildings, or they may be shorter-term ever-changing things like stock and debtors. Assets can also be intangible, that is they are not physical, for instance intellectual property like patents and rights to things.

Balance sheet

The balance sheet is a summary of all the asset, liability and equity accounts at a given point in time. It can be presented in a vertical or horizontal form and with different elements in different places which can be very confusing. The normal UK method now is vertical, listing all the assets then liabilities, and comparing this to equity.

The two halves of the balance sheet (assets and liabilities against equity) can be looked upon as what we own less what we owe on the one side to give a value of net assets. This is then balanced with the source of those net assets which is often equity (or share capital) and accumulated profits.

Budget

It is a common misconception that a budget is just an annual financial forecast. While this is a vital component a budget is a plan for the future. As such it must start with a plan of action for achieving quantifiable objectives. That plan then determines how the financial forecast might look, as that financial forecast is what the outcome will look like if the plan of action is achieved.

The budget is also a vital business management tool as it sets a standard for measuring performance, and provides a tool for coping with foreseeable adverse situations.

Cash book

The cash book is an accounting record of all the transactions through the business bank account.

Typically, with modern accounting systems this is integrated as part of the nominal or general ledger and is not maintained separately.

Creditors

Creditors are amounts the company owes. This would include trade creditors which are amounts owed to suppliers, but creditors would also include amounts due for tax (VAT, PAYE, and Corporation Tax, etc.) and to others that have loaned money to the company. Creditors are often split between those due within one year and those seen as longer term (like bank loans) which are due in over one year.

Debtors

Debtors are the amounts a company is owed. Typically, this is amounts from customers but may also be other amounts such as loans to employees, etc.

Depreciation

Nothing lasts forever... or perhaps not quite. If you have a long-term or fixed asset on your balance sheet that is something that you expect to last many many years, like an item of manufacturing machinery, it will naturally wear out as you use it. Depreciation is an accounting method to reduce the value over the time of its expected life. This also has the impact of recognising a cost of using that asset when calculating profitability.

Double Entry Bookkeeping

A system of accounting for financial transactions accredited to Luca Pacioli a 15th-century mathematician and Franciscan friar. The basic principle is that all transactions must have two equal and opposite elements and therefore all the entries will balance. All entries are recorded in asset, liability, equity, expense, or revenue accounts. An example is perhaps a cash sale. The revenue account is the sale, and the asset account is the bank or cash balance which is now higher as a result of the receipt.

EBIT

Earnings before interest and tax (pronounced as a word: e-bit). Basically, what we know as profit (or net income) but excluding any interest (on debt) costs and taxation. Tends to be a more internationally recognised measure and is now is quite widespread use.

EBITDA

Earnings before interest tax depreciation and amortisation (pronounced as a word: e-bit-daa). This is the same as EBIT but also excludes depreciation and amortisation costs. Why you may ask? Well, there is an argument that this creates a more realistic profit position as it excludes the cost of servicing debt and asset costs. It therefore shows the profit achieved through the trading activity. Again, a very common international measure now.

KPIs

Key Performance Indicators are the key metrics that you need for your business to help you run it better. They can be anything that can be reliably and frequently measured and might cover areas such as sales, production, delivery, customers satisfaction, debt collection, etc. Set alongside a target and the past trends they will let you see what is working and what is not at a glance.

Management accounts v financial accounts

Yes, they are different! And if you are getting good management accounts (often called MI – management information) they should look very different too. But, that said, they add up to the same numbers.

Management accounts, are, well the clue is in the name... the accounts for the management (so tend to stay within your business). They should be presented in such a way that they help you run your business better. They should provide answers and not just raise questions. They should show you what is working, what is not, and where management action is needed, and you should get them monthly and in good time.

Financial accounts on the other hand are normally only produced annually and are in a prescribed format and will be published by filing at Companies House and with the tax authorities. As a management tool they are useless, as a way of benchmarking your business against others they can be very handy.

Margin or Mark-up?

This is all about percentages, and confusing them is a very common mistake that could cost you a lot of money. Margin is often quoted as a percentage of sales. So if you sell something for £100, and the direct cost (the cost of the goods) is £75, you make a margin of £25, or 25% of sales.

So, what is mark-up? This is the amount you increase (mark-up) your cost by to reach your sales figure. So, in the example above our cost is £75, if we mark-up by 33.3% or a third, we get £25, and a sales price of £100.

Nominal ledger

The nominal, or general ledger is the centre of any accounting system. All transactions are recorded in the nominal ledger relating to every financial activity in the business. This would include sales and purchase invoices and various accounting journals necessary to record all other transactions and activities.

Profit and loss account

The profit and loss account (also sometimes called an income or trading statement) shows how the profit (or loss), sometimes known as net income, achieved by the business over a given period is made up. It will therefore start with sales or revenue, less the direct costs of making those sales (cost of sales or cost of goods sold) then deduct other costs like overheads, interest and taxation. The net result is the profit (or loss) and therefore the net increase (or decrease) in the value of the business over that period. This then together with the profits (or losses) from earlier period becomes part of equity on the balance sheet.

Profits and margins

Terminology often gets muddled and different people refer to different profit measures in different ways using the same terms. It can get very confusing. Generally, it is normally the case that margin is the difference between sales (income or revenue) and the direct cost associated with those sales. Direct costs move directly in proportion to sales, and are normally the cost of the goods being sold. Profit (or net income) is normally margin less all other costs or overheads, so the final result of what you have made.

Purchase ledger

As part of the accounting system, the purchase ledger – or bought ledger – is a record of all the amounts that your suppliers are owed by you, invoice by invoice.

Sales ledger

Similar to the purchase ledger, as part of the accounting system, the sales ledger – or debtors ledger – is a record of all the amounts that your customers owe you, invoice by invoice. A common report of the sales ledger position is an aged debtors report showing the totals owed by period in separate columns across the page so at a glance you can see the oldest items and then act on them.

Working capital

Working capital is the oil in the engine of your business. It is in effect the cash (the most liquid of assets) that you need to operate your business properly and effectively. It is calculated as the net total of all your short-term assets less your short-term liabilities. Normally short-term means assets and liabilities that will be liquidated into cash within 12 months. So, in most situations it is stock, work-in-progress, debtors and cash, less creditors.

Further reading

These are some of the business books I consider absolutely essential reading for any serious business owner. While they aren't all, strictly speaking, finance-related, I believe that building your business strategically and building an enterprise that is well-run financially go hand-in-hand.

They're also all pretty good reads. Enjoy!

1. *The E-Myth Revisited: Why Most Small Businesses Don't Work and What To Do About It* by Michael E. Gerber

One of the great misconceptions is that businesses are built by entrepreneurs when in fact most are created by technicians – people who love what they do, and want to run a business around it. The problem is, just because you have the skills and experience to do a particular job, doesn't mean you are any good at running a business that does that technical work.

Gerber advocates building your company as if you were creating a franchise – in other words, a business model which can be repackaged and replicated without needing you, its founder. By creating processes and systems which even the most unqualified employee can follow, you will build a well-polished, professional business that will run just the way you want - and can scale up quickly.

If you read one book on becoming a more efficient business (apart from the one you're now reading!), make it this one.

2. *Stickier Marketing: How to Win Customers In the Digital Age* by Grant Leboff

My bible for how to market your business in the Internet era. Leboff argues that the concept of the unique selling proposition (USP) is ancient history in an age when every idea and everything you say about your company can be copied almost instantly by the competition.

What differentiates you, he says, is not what you do – but how you do it (and who you do it for). Can you give your online fans and followers a unique experience? What emotions are they going to associate with you? How can your marketing get your prospects really involved, instead of simply talking to them?

Leboff does a terrific job of explaining why the Internet has changed marketing, and gives really practical, solid examples of how companies of all sizes can adjust to the challenges.

3. *Start With Why: How Great Leaders Inspire Everyone To Take Action* by Simon Sinek

You know what your business does. But can you articulate why you do it? That is, not just to make money – but what your business's higher purpose is?

Sinek argues that your business won't truly flourish and be exceptional unless you, your employees and clients understand why it exists. This is what inspires. This is what gives a leader charisma and the ability to spark change – not the mechanics of what you do.

Sinek is, in effect, providing a different answer to Leboff's question about how to differentiate our companies in today's market.

This book appeals to me personally, because part of our own work is to help our customers figure out what they really want to achieve with their business, and give them the financial tools to do so. If you don't have time to read this book, make sure you watch Sinek's popular TED talk on the same subject.

4. *The Beermat Entrepreneur: What You Really Need to Know To Turn a Good Idea Into a Great Business* by Mike Southon and Chris West

How do you grow a company, from the moment you think of setting one up, until you sell it?

Southon and West argue that entrepreneurs are mavericks who love good ideas, but find it hard to see them through (if the entrepreneur was in charge of running the back office, they joke, you'd come into work to find an advanced phone system, but no milk in the fridge).

If you want to grow your business, you need to surround yourself with key people in key areas such as sales, production, tech and − of course! − finance (your cornerstones). They can build the right team and create the processes needed for success.

They set out the stages of growth clearly, and give entrepreneurs a practical business-building map that really works. Invaluable.

Acknowledgments

Being a numbers man, words are not really my thing, so making this book a reality has only been possible with the help of a fabulous team of talented people.

My heartfelt thanks go to: Miriam Shaviv and Tony Watts; the Dynamo team led by Steve Richards, particularly Claire Lister and Charly Bailey, who turned my ramblings into something readable; and Tony Herbert at 21st Century Print for producing what you now hold.

I must also thank my team at Insight Associates who always deliver an exceptional service and inspire me on a daily basis. In particular, I would like to thank my Associate Directors, Shirley Hoy and Simon Hammond, who really make things happen and give tremendous commitment, and also the present team including Cara Taylor, Amy Bridger, Natasha Walman and Aaron Edrington.

I am also keen to acknowledge all the key associates that we have worked with over the years. There are too many to mention each one individually but I would like to give special thanks to Keith Steven at KSA Group, and Nick Paterno and Darren Peeling at McBrides. Both have contributed greatly to my personal success and the success of the business.

Also, to all our clients and the businesses I have worked with over the years. Each provides a new learning experience, brings with it fresh challenges and helps us to accumulate the expertise that has made us the successful business that we are today. Many have contributed to this book because of what we have learnt from them. I hope I have given something back to them in this book. Thank you all.

My path would not have led the way it has over the past 25 years without the support of key people along the way, particularly Ann Bright (sadly no longer with us) who started it all with me back in 1992. Also, Sheila Ledain and Claire Ansbridge, who came later, both made staggering contributions.

Finally, to my long-suffering wife Thelma and my exceptionally talented children, Stuart and Amy, thank you. I am so proud of all of you.

And finally...

If reading this tome leaves you wanting more, sign up to my weekly blog for further stories and experiences from real life in the world of business financial management www.InsightBlog.co.uk. Hopefully you will learn, or be reminded of, something useful each week.

And finally, get in touch and discuss your experiences with me at Garry@InsightAssociates.co.uk

I sincerely hope reading this will help you understand those aspects of your own business which may have remained a mystery until now.